LEN GOODMAN

Dancing around Britain

LEN GOODMAN

Dancing around Britain

Trinity Mirror Media

Trinity Mirror Media

DANCING AROUND BRITAIN
By Len Goodman

Editor: Richard Havers
Design: Ben Renshaw, Graeme Helliwell, Michael Perry
Production: Harri Aston
Archive Research: Paul Mason, Vito Inglese
Mirrorpix: Fergus McKenna, Simon Flavin, David Scripps, Clare Hooper

Photography: Mirrorpix, PA Photos, Martin Spaven,
Len Goodman's personal collection
Copyright text: Trinity Mirror Media / Len Goodman

Published by Trinity Mirror Media

Managing Director: Ken Rogers
Publishing Director: Steve Hanrahan
Commercial Director: Will Beedles
Executive Editor: Paul Dove
Executive Art Editor: Rick Cooke
Senior Marketing Executive: Claire Brown
Sales & Marketing Manager: Elizabeth Morgan

First Edition
Published in Great Britain in 2014.
Published and produced by: Trinity Mirror Media,
PO Box 48, Old Hall Street, Liverpool L69 3EB.

ISBN: 9781908695918

Printed and bound by Korotan

"To everyone who loves dancing as much as I do"

Dancing at the Hammersmith Palais in 1960

CONTENTS

A moving journey back in time

If it wasn't for dancing I wouldn't be here to write this book. My dad, who was also named Len, and my mum, Louisa, met at a dance, got married and nine years later along I came. For people of my generation and several before mine, and several after, it was very common for couples to have met at a ballroom somewhere in Britain. It's what you did for entertainment and to meet someone from the opposite sex.

Just like many others from my parents' generation that first got together at a dance, they then went out dancing together. Of course, you couldn't always go dancing, so you went to the pictures sometimes, and what did you go to see? Very often it was films with dancing in them, especially those with the wonderful Fred Astaire and Ginger Rogers. Three decades later I repeated the process, went dancing, then took girls to the cinema, but in my case it was to see West Side Story.

I've made a living from dancing. I've danced, judged dancing – and long before I started doing it on telly – I've taught every kind of dancing, from ballroom to Latin, from formation dancing to disco and I've loved watching dancers on the big and small screens. Dancing has been my life.

For the last one hundred years dancing has been at the heart of the British way of life. We've had dance crazes – good and bad, fashion dictated by dance, and with the coming of Strictly to our TV screens, Saturday night has once again become alright for dancing. Although it's not without controversy as the nation gets up in arms at who should stay and who should go.

Controversy and dancing have long been partners. I recently found this from a newspaper in 1816:

"We remarked with pain that the indecent foreign dance called 'the waltz' was introduced

(we believe for the first time) at the English Court on Friday last. This is a circumstance which ought not to be passed over in silence. National morals depend on national habits; and it is quite sufficient to cast one's eyes on the voluptuous intertwining of the limbs, and close compressure of the bodies, in their dance, to see that it is indeed far removed from the modest reserve, which has hitherto been distinctive of English females. So long as this obscene display was confined to prostitutes and adulteresses we did not think it deserving of notice; but now that it is attempted to be forced on respectable classes of society by the civil example of their superiors we feel it a duty to warn every parent against exposing his daughter to so fatal a contagion.

"We owe a due deference to superiors in rank, but we owe a higher duty to morality. We know not how it has happened (probably by the recommendation of some worthless and ignorant French dancing master) that so indecent a dance has now been exhibited at the English court, but the novelty is one deserving of severe reprobation, and we trust it will never again be tolerated in any moral English society."

I've taught a lot of people to waltz in my time, but I never looked upon it as corrupting the nation's morals.

In a little book I was recently given called, Ballroom & Services Dance Instructor (wartime edition) it says: "Do not assume, if you are a keen dancer, that dancing is the begin-all and end-all of life; your partner may have accomplishments in another sphere."

It's true of course, but dancing has been my life and it's great to be able to share some of my memories with you.

Ken Freedman

Ballroom dancing at the old Assembly Rooms in Newcastle in the 1950s

My nervous first steps on road to a life of dancing

If it wasn't for football I probably would have been like everyone else and just gone dancing so I could meet girls. It's what we all did back in the 1950s…and what my parents' generation did too. Of course, I ended up dancing professionally and teaching people to dance, long before I ever got on the TV and started telling celebrities how to do it. Let me take you back and tell you how it all began…

Everybody has to start somewhere...

I was no different to many people of my generation in that I started getting interested in dancing around the same time as I was getting interested in girls – I was about fourteen.

Some of my mates started going to the Court School of Dancing in Welling in Kent. I never fancied it much, as I was more interested in playing football and running. Once I plucked up the courage to go it was the start of a ritual. It began with a hair cut, because going dancing meant you needed to be smart. Close to where I lived was a hairdressers called Maison Maurice, it was the place where all the lads went for a cut, friction and blow-dry. I would go on a Wednesday night for mine, having walked straight there from school. Barry was the man to have cut your hair as he did the best 'Boston', the

Above *Dancing at the Blackheath youth club in March 1959*

Right *A dance called 'the creep' being performed at the Royal Theatre in Tottenham in 1953*

➤

straight across cut at the back. Once Barry had finished the cut he would massage this stuff into your hair – the friction bit – and then he would blow it into shape. It cost two bob, or maybe two and sixpence, but it was money well spent because you looked the bee's knees.

Then it was home for a bath – we didn't have a shower, that was far too fancy. I'd then get dressed in my best clobber and meet up with Pete and some of the other lads before heading off to the Court School of Dancing, which was next to the Granada cinema in the High Street. Being mid-week, and still being young teenagers, it wasn't a late night. We started at 7pm and it finished at 9pm. It was called a 'teen and twenty single mingle' but there was no twenties, it was all school kids from about thirteen to maybe sixteen years old.

Below *If only I'd been this confident. Joanna Dunham and Alan Bates in Cafe de Artistes in Chelsea researching a play in which they were to appear in 1958*

Right *A couple taking a break from the dancing at the Hammersmith Palais in 1947*

It wasn't like you would imagine nowadays with fifty girls and three blokes, it was much more evenly matched than that. First there was a bit of instruction for about half an hour with the boys on one side of the room and the girls over the other side. Eventually, you partnered up, which was the worst bit for me. I found the whole thing very nerve-racking. I was very shy and had not really been in contact with girls – apart for my cousin Marilyn who I'd seen naked, but that was in 1950 when I was six.

"Ok, now find yourself a partner," said the instructor. I hung back, which meant the choice wasn't that great. When you're fourteen going on fifteen, who you're dancing with really matters. Everyone had paired up and there were a few more girls than men and before I could get my act together a girl came over and got hold of me. Next thing I knew I was dancing around doing the quickstep – well after a fashion. For the rest of the evening it was more of a free dance but to begin with I was a bit stuck, as I had to wait until a quickstep came on, as it was the only dance I vaguely knew.

As the weeks went by, and I got to grips with more of the dances, things improved. I sort of learned the basics of the waltz, the foxtrot, the cha cha cha and the jive. But even so, I was still slow to ask girls to dance on account of my shyness. As the weeks went by I got better at dancing and after some embarrassing incidents with various girls, I got to know a girl called Sally and we sort of started going out together.

"'OK, NOW FIND YOURSELF A PARTNER,' SAID THE INSTRUCTOR. I HUNG BACK, WHICH MEANT THE CHOICE WASN'T THAT GREAT. WHEN YOU'RE FOURTEEN GOING ON FIFTEEN, WHO YOU'RE DANCING WITH REALLY MATTERS"

➤

I eventually asked her to come with me to the Embassy Ballroom on a Saturday night; this despite the fact that you needed to be sixteen to get in. 'No One Under Sixteen Allowed, by order of the Management' read the large sign on the window of the entry booth. "Are you sure you're sixteen son?"

"'Course I am. I've been an apprentice for a year."

"Okay, this time I'll believe you. It's 1/6 each, so that's three bob for the two of you."

Thankfully, this was way before anyone had thought of ID cards for teenagers.

Compared to the Court School of Dancing, which was about the size of a very large front room, this was like Buckingham Palace. The Embassy held maybe three hundred people on the dance floor, it had a chrome and glass foyer, flock wall paper, even a silhouette of a lady's head and one of a man's head on the doors of the toilets. The urinals were the poshest I'd ever been in. Added to which the Embassy had a dance band, a kind of poor man's Joe Loss, but it was a hell of a lot better than the records we danced to at the Court. Most important of all it had a glitter ball. Not that we had too long to enjoy all this as Sally still had to be home by ten o'clock. When I eventually took her home I got into all sorts of trouble, but we'll leave that for another time.

I hadn't gone to the Court School of Dancing or the Embassy Ballroom because of any real love of dancing, there was no desire on my part to take it seriously. I went because that's where you met girls and that was my mission. To be honest it was the same for all my mates; it could have been dancing, bowling or even flower arranging if that's how you met girls and got to go out with them. I was doing what hundreds of thousands of kids across the country were doing.

This was at the end of the 1950s, as more traditional forms of dancing seemed to be giving way to rock and roll in a big way. But just like my parents' generation it was dancing that allowed me to get up close and personal with the opposite sex.

The final of the Welsh Open Professional Dancing Championships at the Top Rank in Cardiff in June 1967. Many people enjoyed less traditional forms of dancing such as rock and roll, inset

From Hackney Marches to Erith in one quickstep

In the early 1960s, ballroom dancing didn't really appeal to me, despite my dad trying to get me to go with him and my step mum. I was more interested in playing football to be honest. But then disaster struck, I broke a metatarsal bone in my foot – the same one that Wayne Rooney broke. I was playing on Hackney Marshes when it happened. I kicked the ball north while at the same time the biggest centre-half in the world – well that's my story and I'm sticking to it – tried to kick the ball south. The outcome was my foot went west and I was in agony. I was hobbling around for weeks, which certainly put paid to any thoughts of going dancing.

The solution, according to my doctor, was to take up ballroom dancing, which is how come I ended up at Erith Dance Studio, wearing a slipper on my dodgy foot and shuffling around the floor. Before all that I was first shown how to hold my partner – the five points of contact for the perfect ballroom hold. Maybe it was just me but I got very confused because it was two ladies showing us. Which lady was the man and which was the lady? Eventually, I got the gist of the grip and the ladies came around adjusting our arms and our body positions.

Having loosely mastered the hold and the step, next came the rise and fall. The waltz should have a gentle rise and fall, well my left leg was no problem – it had a lovely rise and fall – but my right leg was all fall and no rise. I looked like a man trying to dance with one leg in the gutter and the other on the pavement. As my foot got better I began to find I actually quite liked it.

The Erith Dance Studio was on two floors right above Burton's, the gentleman's tailor. Our classes were on the

Above That's me, top right, when I played for my work's apprentices football team

Right Queen Elizabeth II dancing with Air Marshall Sir John Baldwin at the Light Brigade Balacava Centenary Ball at the Hyde Park Hotel in 1954. Back then if you couldn't dance properly there was no way that you would get on!

➤

➤

first floor and on the floor above that was where Henry Kingston used to teach. I say teach but in actual fact he was a coach, not a teacher. In dancing a coach is well above a teacher. Neither was he just any old coach, but a top coach. Henry and Joy Tolhurst had been dance partners and were also married. They had been one of the top couples in the dance world for many years but Henry was an even better coach than he was a dancer.

Amongst those he coached were Bill and Bobbie Irvine, who were world champions at the time, Richard Gleave and Janet Wade, who became amateur world champions along with Anthony Hurley and Fay Sexton, who would also go on to become professional champions. At the end of his coaching sessions he would come downstairs to our studio to check out his diary that he kept behind the tea bar in the corner. As soon as he came in everyone tried to dance a little better. It was like a silent voice had called out – "Henry Kingston's in the house!" Everybody would suddenly stand a little straighter and try their hardest not to make a mistake. It was not that he ever said anything or was unpleasant; far from it, he was a charming man. As a former world champion he just had an aura about him.

One evening, while we were learning the waltz, Henry Kingston appeared in the room along with two couples. Naturally, everyone's elbows got a little straighter; I certainly tried standing a little taller with my head more erect.

"I'd like to introduce Bill and Bobbie Irvine." He went on to explain their many achievements and then said:

"Billy and Bobbie are going to show you a quickstep." He nodded to Pauline who put the needle on the record of the big record player in the opposite corner of the studio from the tea bar – they began dancing beautifully to a Victor Sylvester record.

➤

"ONE EVENING, WHILE WE WERE LEARNING THE WALTZ, HENRY KINGSTON APPEARED IN THE ROOM ALONG WITH TWO COUPLES. NATURALLY, EVERYONE'S ELBOWS GOT A LITTLE STRAIGHTER"

Opposite *Cherry Kingston and me doing a demonstration dance. During the 1970s we were doing up to 200 of these a year around Britain*

Left *Janet Wade and her husband Richard Gleave after winning the Scottish Open Amateur Dancing Championship at the Locarno Ballroom in Glasgow shortly before I first met them in Erith*

I, and probably everyone else, was captivated. I recalled seeing them before but this time I had an appreciation of just how brilliant they were. After the quickstep they stopped and Bill Irvine spoke to us. He was a Scotsman and had a lovely lilt to his voice.

"Good evening, ladies and gentleman. That, of course, was the quickstep and now we would like to demonstrate the tango." Bobbie stood beside him, she was the most elegant and sophisticated looking woman I had ever seen in the flesh. I later found out that she was South African, while Bill had been a milkman before he became a professional dancer – perhaps he worked with Sean Connery.

After about six weeks it was announced that in a further six weeks we would be able to take our bronze medal in the waltz and quickstep. By this point I was no longer dancing under doctor's orders, my foot was well on the way to total recovery; I'd given Dad back his slipper and I was back into a pair of ordinary shoes, but not winkle pickers which are not ideal for ballroom dancing. I found I actually enjoyed myself, I looked forward to going and sitting around the edge of the studio waiting for my class to begin I was now all eager anticipation. I was on my way to becoming a proper dancer…

"I LOOKED FORWARD TO GOING AND SITTING AROUND THE EDGE OF THE STUDIO WAITING FOR MY CLASS TO BEGIN I WAS NOW ALL EAGER ANTICIPATION. I WAS ON MY WAY TO BECOMING A PROPER DANCER…"

This was taken in the late 1950s at a club in London. It could just as easily be me sitting around watching what was happening on the dance floor

Morris dancers from Coventry giving a display on the green outside Kenilworth Castle in June 1960

CHAPTER 2

Jazzing up our big nights out

No-one quite knows when people first danced. Maybe it was cavemen! Every society throughout history has danced, in one way or another. In earlier times dancing was done for the entertainment of the rich, but then people began dancing with one another for their own enjoyment. Take Morris dancing, it's a tradition that goes back hundreds of years. It was around the time of the First World War, and shortly thereafter, that people started dancing together for enjoyment in public places. It was the coming of the jazz age that got everyone excited about dancing on a Saturday night...

Going jazz crazy...

As far as entertainment is concerned two things happened after the First World War ended. There was the widespread appeal of jazz, which crossed the Atlantic from America and excited people the length and breadth of Britain. The other was the coming of the phonograph as a means of playing records at home and in smaller public places. It meant that it was not necessary to have a band or someone who could play the piano in order to dance.

Later in the 1920s along came the BBC and the wireless. To begin with there was nothing as frivolous as dance music on the radio – heaven forbid. But quickly that all changed and regular dance band shows were broadcast from famous hotels and other venues in London and further afield.

The Original Dixieland Jazz Band was the first jazz band to make a record in February 1917 and soon its records and others made their way across the Atlantic, in part thanks to American

Above *Glasgow's Locarno dance hall in the early 1920s*

Below *The Original Dixieland Jazz Band*

servicemen. By the spring of 1918, American officers on leave in Britain from the trenches in France were showing off, according to the newspapers, what was called the Jazz Trot. It was, in the words of one Mayfair club hostess, "healthy and harmless. Half the brides of Mayfair have met their men at dance teas".

After 1942 it was often said American servicemen who came to Britain were "overfed, oversexed and over here" – seems like they were in the First World War too! It was around the time of the war that the foxtrot was 'invented', probably named after its inventor, Harry Fox.

The Original Dixieland Jazz Band also came to Britain, arriving on a liner at Liverpool in April 1919. With the fashion for jazz dancing, the band's assertion that they were the 'originators of jazz', along with their performances at the London Hippodrome and even an audience before King George V, meant that they were guaranteed publicity. But they were not the first jazz band to play in Britain.

There was Dawkin's Famous Coloured Jazz Band who performed in Scotland in March 1919; this was a group of West Indian musicians led by Oscar Dawkins, a drummer. Also, 'The Jazz Seven, the sensation of London and Paris' was playing at the Alhambra Theatre in Leith, Edinburgh's port area in March. By late April, the American Varsity Jazz Band was also in Britain. Us Brits went crazy for jazz.

"TO BEGIN WITH THERE WAS NOTHING AS FRIVOLOUS AS DANCE MUSIC ON THE RADIO – HEAVEN FORBID"

ARMISTICE DAY ANNIVERSARY.
TO THE DANCE — TO-NIGHT.

NO better way of celebrating the return of Joy-Day!
Europe's finest dancing salon promises a merry
night at the Fancy Dress Carnival arranged for your
enjoyment.

JOSE COLLINS & GEORGE GRAVES
will be there, and will present six valuable prizes—two
to those who best impersonate them in their stage
successes, and the others for the best costumes.

Two Bands: The Original Dixie Land Jazz Band and
Melody Mixers—the best in the world.
Eighty Lady and Gentlemen Instructors.

GRAND FANCY DRESS CARNIVAL
from 8 to 2.30
ADMISSION - 7/6

PALAIS DE DANSE
THE TALK OF LONDON HAMMERSMITH

Easily accessible from all ports of London by tube or bus.
Within two minutes of Hammersmith District and Underground Stations.
A.P.S.

EDINBURGH SUBSCRIPTION DANCES
FREEMASONS' HALL
To-night at 8.30
Also 13th, 20th, and 27th March.
SPECIAL "JAZZ" BAND
Double Ticket, £1 1 0. Single Ticket, 12/6.
Dance Director—Mr D. G. MacLennan.
Business Management—Methven Simpson, Ltd.

Right and below
Jazz musicians entertain dancers on a Saturday night at the Hammersmith Palais

Opposite
A jazz festival pulls in a large crowd

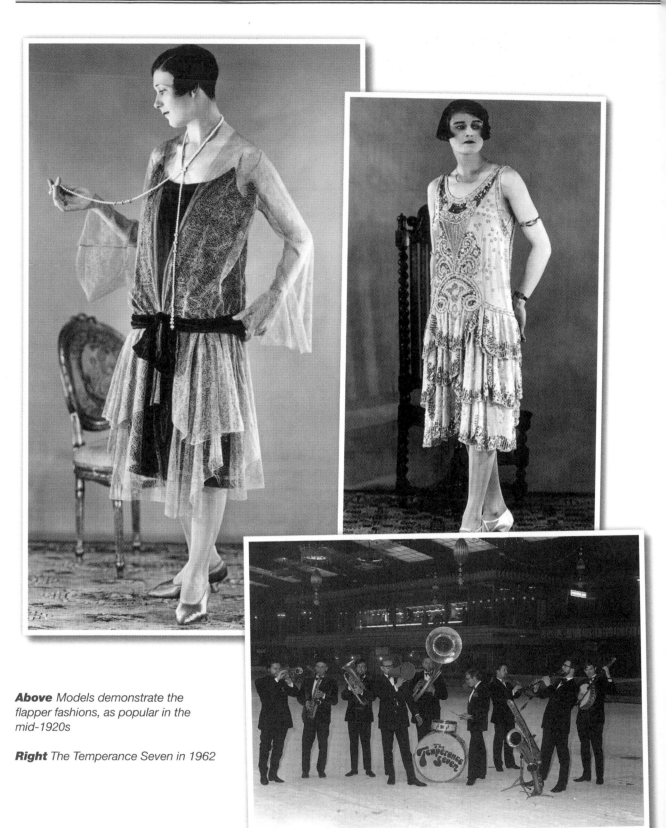

Above Models demonstrate the flapper fashions, as popular in the mid-1920s

Right The Temperance Seven in 1962

The Charleston

Like most people my age and younger I think I first became aware of the Charleston dance in 1961 when a band named The Temperance Seven had a hit record with a song of the same name. They had already had a No.1 with You're Driving Me Crazy and a top ten hit with Pasadena. They celebrated the 1920s in their dress and their style of music. It was a time when trad jazz was all the rage in Britain, a time when Acker Bilk, Kenny Ball and Chris Barber were also very popular.

I found out years later that George Martin had produced the Temperance Seven records; this was just a year or so before he auditioned The Beatles and their arrival on the scene changed everything for modern pop music.

The Charleston, written in 1923, and the dance that it created were named after a city in South Carolina in the southern states of America. The songwriter was a pianist named James P. Johnson, who played what's called a stride piano. The song first came to prominence as a result of a Broadway show and, by 1926, the dance had became a sensation.

Johnson took his inspiration for the music from watching dancers in Harlem and it was taken to a whole new level by dancers in this part of New York when Johnson's music was recorded. They introduced the fast kicking step – kicking their feet, both forward and backward. In the 1930s the Charleston was an inspiration for what became the Lindy Hop. Whereas the Charleston was the perfect dance for the hot jazz of the 1920s played by everyone from Louis Armstrong to the Harlem Hot Shots, the Lindy Hop is more associated with the swing bands of the 1930s.

The dance gets its name from American aviator Charles Lindbergh's nickname of 'Lindy' – he was the first aviator to fly solo across the Atlantic – his hop took place in 1927.

The first reference to the dance I could find in the Daily Mirror was in July 1925 when, in the section called Ladies' Mirror, it was announced that: "Annette Mills and Robert Sielle gave such a nice party at the Carnival Club to show us how to do the new Charleston dance, which is extremely fascinating and will very soon be danced in all first-class ballroom."

It went on to say that it made the foxtrot seem dull by comparison. "It is so sprightly and vivacious, and an excellent 'reducer', I should imagine." A reducer? A bit like a modern day Zumba class!

Josephine Baker doing the Charleston at the Folies Bergère, Paris, in 1926

Big band Britain

Bandleader and trumpeter Jack Jackson performing with his band in 1938

During the 1930s there were well over one thousand professional dance bands in Britain. Add to these the thousands of semi-pro and amateur bands and the number of musicians playing live music on a regular basis was colossal, and much of what they played was for dancing. The craze for hot jazz that spread from America took hold in Britain and while British bands may not have been as big, and in some cases as exciting, as their American counterparts, they were extremely professional and they were what the nation danced to.

These days with amplification and high powered speakers, it is sometimes easy to forget that back in the 1930s there was no way of playing music loud enough in a ballroom or even fairly modest hall to allow for dancing. It had to be a band and the very best of these also secured spots on the radio, where they broadcast from famous hotels and other night spots on the BBC.

> **"IT IS EASY TO FORGET THAT BACK IN THE 1930S THERE WAS NO WAY OF PLAYING MUSIC LOUD ENOUGH IN A BALLROOM OR EVEN A FAIRLY MODEST HALL TO ALLOW FOR DANCING"**

Check out any old newspaper from the 1930s and there will be dance bands playing every night. The BBC Dance Orchestra, directed by Henry Hall, broadcast every weekday at 5.15 and other regulars were Jack Hylton's Orchestra and Maurice Winnick and his Orchestra. There were also orchestras from places such as London's Hotel Victoria, the Savoy Hotel, The Waldorf Hotel and the Café Colette.

Newspapers carried listings of dance music being broadcast on foreign radio stations in Holland, Germany, Poland, Hungary and Denmark; dance music was everywhere. Additionally, the BBC broadcast regular shows of 'Dance Records'. The point of all this is that dance music was pop music, just as it has been since records first appeared. Pop is not so much a style of music as short for 'popular' – every era has its own pop music and in the 1930s it was music to dance to.

The big-name bandleaders were to begin with bigger stars than the singers that worked for them. Bert Ambrose, who worked under just his surname, was extremely popular. He started out in London's Embassy club in the early 1920s and by the 1930s he had a residency at London's Mayfair Hotel before he opened his own club that he called Ciros. It was Ambrose who gave Vera Lynn a job as his singer in 1937, earlier he had employed both Sam Browne, Elsie Carlisle, Denny Denis and Evelyn Dall. Another big name was Geraldo, whose

"DANCE MUSIC WAS POP MUSIC. POP IS NOT SO MUCH A STYLE AS SHORT FOR 'POPULAR' – EVERY ERA HAS ITS OWN POP MUSIC AND IN THE 1930S IT WAS MUSIC TO DANCE TO"

Ballrooms often had theme nights and shown here is the Beach Night Dancing contest at the Locarno Ballroom in Streatham in August 1932

➤

real name was Gerald Brigh. He had begun his career as a pianist for silent movies but by the 1930s he was leading his own orchestra.

Carroll Gibbons was an American who made his name in Britain when in 1924 he led the Savoy Orpheans, a band that became one of the biggest names in London and the rest of Britain. By the 1930s Gibbons was also broadcasting regularly on Radio Luxembourg.

Henry Hall's big opportunity came in the early 1920s when he secured a position with London Midland and Scottish Railway to take charge of the music in their hotels; their large chain of properties included

Right BBC's Broadcasting House – which was central to the scene's development

Below A section from the front cover of sheet music for The Savoy Orpheans. Sheet music sales were huge during the 1930s

PLAYED, RECORDED, AND BROADCASTED BY THE FAMOUS

SAVOY ORPHEANS BAND.
OF THE SAVOY HOTEL, LONDON.

FAMOUS RADIO STARS
HENRY HALL

FAMOUS RADIO STARS
JACK HYLTON

Henry Hall, Jack Hylton and Jack Payne were three of the most influential figures in the development of big band music in Britain

FAMOUS RADIO STARS
JACK PAYNE

"IT IS DIFFICULT PERHAPS FOR PEOPLE TODAY TO RECOGNISE JUST HOW POPULAR BANDLEADERS WERE IN PRE-WAR BRITAIN"

Gleneagles Hotel in Scotland, where Hall led the band. In 1924 he persuaded the BBC to broadcast his band live from Gleneagles and this was the start of his long and fruitful relationship with the corporation.

In 1932 he took over the BBC Dance Orchestra from Jack Payne. Hall even took his orchestra on the maiden voyage of the Queen Mary; it is difficult perhaps for people today to recognise just how popular bandleaders were in pre-war Britain.

Jack Hylton, having been a musician in the Army during the First World War, started his own band in the early 1920s and by 1923 was recording records under his own name. Hylton was probably the bandleader who was most influenced by American jazz. He brought Louis Armstrong to Britain to play, as well as the leading jazz saxophonist, Coleman Hawkins.

Trumpeter Jack Jackson played with Hylton's band before joining Jack Payne's band in 1931 before then forming his own orchestra in 1933. Almost immediately he secured a residency at London's Dorchester Hotel that lasted for five years. After the Second World War he worked on the BBC and his programmes of music that he punctuated with comedy clips was always one of my favourites, right up until it ended in 1977.

Other big names that started their careers as bandleaders include Joe Loss, who started at the Astoria Ballroom in London and then worked at the famous Kit-Cat Club. Ray Noble started a band in Britain then moved to America and for a while in 1934 Glenn Miller played trombone in his orchestra. He even appeared in Hollywood musical films including Here We Go Again. Then there was Billy Cotton, Oscar Rabin, Harry Roy, Lew Stone, Jay Wilbur and Fred Elizalde… every one a

The GEC ballroom in
Coventry in 1935

➤

household name in pre-war Britain. I got a lovely letter from a lady named Patricia Price who was 90 years young as I was putting this book together. She grew up in Birmingham and remembers this era well. She wrote:

"I envied the older girls, I was still at school, arriving at the Palace Ballroom in Erdington. The idea of dancing was forbidden to me as my father, even in the 1930s, was still of the opinion that there was something decadent about young men putting their arms around young ladies; naturally this taboo only added to the appeal.

"I watched enviously as the girls alighted from the tram … their aim was to look like Betty Grable or Ginger Rogers, depending on the film being shown at the local cinemas. The boys were equally fastidious. Lounge suits with collar and tie were the order of the day. Prior to the war, the LMS Railway ran a train from New Street station at the weekend. It was called The Dance Special and left Birmingham at 4.30pm and arrived in Blackpool at

"I WAS TREMBLING, PARTLY THROUGH EXCITEMENT AND PARTLY NERVOUSNESS"

7.30pm. The train returned from Blackpool at 11.30pm. There were afternoon tea dances at the Palace on Wednesday and Saturday – most shops in Birmingham closed on Wednesday afternoon. My first venture into this wonderland was on a Saturday when I was about 15; my father agreed as my friend's sister came along as a chaperone.

"I remember to this day as we entered the ballroom, it was probably Cyril Slaughter and his Orchestra, playing Blue Skies. I was trembling, partly through excitement and partly nervousness."

Left The annual Lyons 'Big Bang' held at the Hammersmith Palais in January 1937

Above Dancing in the 'Palais' on the pier at Clacton-on-Sea, June 1934

Above These women were singing along to jazz songs in 1929

Left Ennis Hylton, the wife of bandleader Jack Hylton, at a rehearsal with the band in 1933

Right Robert Lindsay and Emma Thompson starring in the musical Me And My Girl in 1985

The Lambeth Walk

At the height of the pre-war big band era along came a song that had much more to do with London and the kind of East End culture that my family knew all about – it was The Lambeth Walk.

Its music is by Noel Gay and the words are by Douglas Furber and L. Arthur Rose and it featured in the 1937 musical Me And My Girl. Lambeth is not far from where my family had the barrow in the market and the musical was all about a cockney barrow boy who inherited an earldom and then almost loses his Lambeth girlfriend.

The dance became really popular in East London after Lupino Lane recorded The Lambeth Walk following his appearance in the stage play. In 1939 Lupino appeared in a film called The Lambeth Walk.

The number in the stage musical was a real show-stopper with colourful cockney characters dancing in a way similar to Dick Van Dyke in Mary Poppins.

It was not only popular in London. I It even crossed the Atlantic and Duke Ellington recorded it and had a top ten hit in 1938. Meanwhile, in Germany, the Nazi party saw the song as evil Jewish propaganda and tried to ban it, unsuccessfully as it turned out, and it remained popular throughout the war – proving that you cannot keep a good song down!

Big band America

I f Britain had a vibrant big band scene it was nothing compared to America, where there were over ten thousand bands spread throughout the country. Among the biggest of the big-name bandleaders are Tommy and Jimmy Dorsey, Count Basie, Benny Goodman, Les Brown, Duke Ellington, Woody Herman, Glen Miller, Artie Shaw, Paul Whiteman and Harry James – all names that came to epitomise this glamorous era.

The big bands were first and foremost dance bands and their zenith ran from about 1935 to the early 1950s. Changing tastes, the birth of rock 'n' roll and the advent of television all played a part in their waning popularity.

The importance of the big bands lay not just in their role of 'introducing' a number of important singers, but in the fact that they bridged the gap between hot jazz, as popularised by men like Louis Armstrong and Jelly Roll Morton in the 1920s, and a more 'acceptable' style of playing. For white Middle America the big bands were a

window on black rhythms, a chance to listen to a 'jazzier' style of playing without crossing the line. The big bands lifted jazz from the roughest dance halls and brothels to the supper clubs, nightclubs and even the concert hall frequented by a more affluent audience.

Jimmy Dorsey and trumpeter Bunny Berigan came to Britain in 1930 and they inspired British bands. Bands like Louis Armstrong's in the 1920s would have typically been five or seven strong, which is why the bands that began to find prominence in the 1930s were called big bands. Generally, they were about 15-strong but could be as large as 25 and as small as 10.

By the mid 1930s they generally consisted of three trumpets, three trombones, four saxophones and a four-piece rhythm section (drums, double bass, guitar and piano). To this a couple of clarinets were sometimes added.

A decade later a typical band had grown to four trombones, four trumpets, five saxophones and a four-piece rhythm section. Some bandleaders experimented with French horns, flutes and even violins. Not every band from the 1920s was small. Paul Whiteman led an impressive and large band throughout the decade, more of a show band than a dance band; Bing Crosby and the Rhythm Boys got their break with Whiteman.

Today, we are so used to groups of musicians using amplification to beef up their sound that many people have never ever seen or heard a big band in all their real life glory. In the ballrooms, clubs, hotels and theatres of the late 1930s it must have been a revelation for audiences. Not least because the reproduction quality of radios and gramophones during that decade failed miserably to do justice to the excitement and power of a large live band in full cry. For the singers it must have been a wonderful feeling to be 'out front' as the band laid down their musical accompaniment.

Opposite *Duke Ellington in London in 1935, top left, and jazz legend Louis Armstrong*

Below *The Barnstormers playing at the Barn Club in Barnet in 1933*

Frankie Satin?

Among the singers who found prominence with the big bands was Frank Sinatra, who has always been one of my favourite singers. Frank Sinatra joined Harry James in June 1939; their most famous recording was All Or Nothing At All, which they cut in August 1939. Shortly after they first met, Sinatra and Harry James had a disagreement. James felt that Sinatra was not the ideal name for his new singer, it was too Italian. He told Frank he should change it and call himself Frankie Satin. "Change it? You kiddin?" is how Frank's reply has been reported, or perhaps paraphrased. Many years later Frank said: "If I'd done that, I'd be working cruise ships today."

A month after Frank Sinatra joined the Harry James band he was heard for the first time in Britain, inevitably on the BBC. It was on July 19, 1939, that the Harry James band broadcast on the radio. Reporter Mike Butcher tuned in not expecting much, as he had been unimpressed with Harry's records. "You'll understand how pleasantly surprised I was when between a real killer-diller workout on Beer Barrel Polka and some similarly depressing manifestations of the swing era's worst aspects, a male singer announced as Frank Sinatra came on with the sentimentally affecting From The Bottom Of My Heart and To You."

Not long after the Second World War broke out, Sinatra joined Tommy Dorsey's band and the rest is history…

A poster promoting top American trumpeter Harry James, top; Ol' Blue Eyes himself, below left; and Tommy Dorsey, bottom right

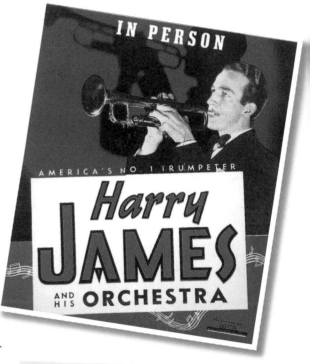

Dance crazes came and went in the 1930s almost as quickly as they did in the post-war era. This one was called The Big Apple, a variation on Lindy Hop. This is Louise Kline and Bill Ball at London's Trocadero Restaurant in October 1937

➤

Other singers with the big bands included Fred Astaire with Leo Reisman's band – people forget what a good singer Astaire was, probably because he was such a brilliant dancer. Doris Day sang with Bob Crosby and the Les Brown band. Peggy Lee with Benny Goodman, Dinah Washington with Lionel Hampton and Sarah Vaughan with Billy Eckstine's band.

Above Doris Day

Top right Singer and actress Peggy Lee

Right Bandleader Lionel Hampton at the Empress Hall in London

"DORIS DAY SANG WITH BOB CROSBY AND THE LES BROWN BAND, PEGGY LEE WITH BENNY GOODMAN, DINAH WASHINGTON WITH LIONEL HAMPTON"

American jazz performer Benny Goodman, pictured above rehearsing for a concert at the Albert Hall and, left, playing his clarinet with his new British band at the King's Head in Acton, London, in the early 1970s

DANCE BANDS AND THEIR THEME SONGS

Every dance band had their theme songs, some that have become very popular in their own right and all were great to dance to!

Ambrose & His Orchestra
When Day Is Over

Andy Kirk & His Clouds Of Joy
Clouds

Artie Shaw Orchestra
Nightmare

Ben Pollock Band
Song Of The Islands

Benny Goodman Orchestra
Let's Dance

Bert Lown Orchestra
Bye Bye Blues

Bill Cotton Band
Somebody Stole My Gal

Bob Crosby Orchestra
Summertime

Bunny Berigan Orchestra
I Can't Get Started With You

Cab Calloway
Minnie The Moocher

Carroll Gibbons & His Savoy Orpheans
On The Air

Charlie Barnet Orchestra
Redskin Rhumba

Charlie Spivak Orchestra
Star Dreams

Chick Webb Orchestra
I May Be Wrong

Claude Thornhill Band
Snowfall

Count Basie Orchestra
One O'Clock Jump

Desi Arnez Orchestra
Cuban Pete

Duke Ellington Orchestra
Take The A Train

Eddie Duchin Orchestra
My Twilight Dreams

Fletcher Henderson Orchestra
Christopher Columbus

Gene Krupa Orchestra
Apurksody/Starburst

Geraldo & His Orchestra
Lady Of Spain

Glen Gray & the Casa Loma Orchestra
Smoke Rings

Glen Miller Orchestra
Moonlight Serenade

Guy Lombardo Orchestra
Auld Lang Syne

Hal Kemp Orchestra
How I'll Miss You When Summer Is Gone

Harry James Orchestra
Ciribiribin

Harry Roy Orchestra
Bugle Call Rag

Horace Heidt Orchestra
I'll Love You In My Dreams

Ina Ray Hutton & Her Orchestra
Gotta Have Your Love

Jack Hylton Orchestra
Oh, Listen To The Band

Jack Teagarden & His Orchestra
I've Got A Right To Sing The Blues

Jan Garber Orchestra
My Dear

Jan Savitt Band
Quaker City Jazz/It's A Wonderful World

Jimmie Lunceford Orchestra
Jazznocracy/Uptown Blues

Jimmy Dorsey Orchestra
Contrasts

Kay Kyser Orchestra
Thinking Of You

Leo Reisman & his Orchestra
What Is This Thing Called Love

Les Brown Orchestra
Leap Frog

Lional Hampton Orchestra
Flying Home

Nobble Sissle Band
Hello Sweatheart, Hello

Paul Whiteman Orchestra
Rhapsody in Blue

Ray Anthony & his Orchestra
Young Man With A Horn

Ray Noble Band
I'll See You In My dreams/Midnight moon

Red Nichols Band
Parade Of The Five Pennies

Red Norvo Orchestra
Surrender Dear

Stan Kenton Orchestra
Artistry In Rhythm

Ted Heath Orchestra
Listen To My Music

Tommy Dorsey Orchestra
I'm Getting Sentimental Over You

Vaughn Monroe Orchestra
Racing With The Moon

Vincent Lopez Orchestra
Nola

Woody Herman Orchestra
Blue Prelude/Blue Flame

Xavier Cugat Orchestra
My Shawl

Knees Up Mother Brown

This is one of those songs that I will forever associate with my East End childhood; going to the pub and hearing people sing this round the piano and before long half of them would be dancing. The song's title isn't so much about lifting your knees up as it is about a party or dance, cockney slang for a right good time!

The song's origins go back to the end of the First World War and it seems to have been popular around the time of the Armistice on November 11, 1918. Strangely, the song was not published until 1938 and during the Second World War it became very popular, with Elsie and Doris Waters performing it regularly on the radio.

In the 1960s it became the inspiration for the song Step In Time performed by Dick Van Dyke and the chorus of Victorian Chimney sweeps in the movie, Mary Poppins.

SONGS THAT GOT BRITAIN DANCING

Women dancing outside a house during the Second World War and, right, people celebrating the Armistice in 1918

SONGS THAT GOT BRITAIN DANCING

An example of the hokey cokey and, right, Jimmy Kennedy, pictured on the left

The Hokey Cokey

This is one of those songs that we probably all think is a lot older than it really is – I certainly did.

Its origins lay in war-torn London during the Blitz. A Canadian Army officer suggested to British dance band leader Al Tabor that he write a song that could be danced to in a similar way to Under The Spreading Chestnut Tree, a number for dancing to, with actions.

Tabor found his inspiration from a young lad selling ice-cream in the street who was shouting, "Hokey pokey penny a lump. Have a lick make you jump." According to legend it was the Canadian who changed it to Cokey as it meant crazy back home.

After it was written there appears to be some kind of legal wrangle with the well-known songwriter and music publisher, Jimmy Kennedy; an out-of-court settlement saw Kennedy ending up with the rights to the composition.

The argument has raged on ever since as to who wrote what and letters were even written to The Times about its origins. In actual fact the dance actions of "right hand in, left hand in" and all the other permutations go way, way back. Recently, it came to light that a book published in the 19th century had similar words.

It's likely that it goes back even further than that and is an example of a dance that would have been done at local get-togethers, maybe as far back as the 1600s. Interestingly, different countries have slightly different versions of the lyrics and in some countries it even has a slightly different title.

At Christmas 1981 it even made the charts when a group calling themselves The Snowmen took it to No.18. Rumour has it that it's Ian Dury on vocals, but people are unsure. Many think it is in fact Jona Lewie, an artist fond of both Christmas records and novelty hits under a pseudonym (he was also Terry Dactyl & the Dinosaurs).

Miss Dorene Hare, the well known compere of the Shipmates Ashore programme at the Merchant Navy Club, dancing with one of the Merchant Navy members who attended the recording to her theme tune Sailor Sail Me Round in July 1943. You have to remember, this was way before my time!

CHAPTER 3

Refusing to skip a beat even as the bombs fell down

There are few things that can lift the spirits like music and dancing, and throughout the Second World War it was amazing just how many people actually did go dancing. Once the Americans had entered the war they brought their music with them and it was in the summer of 1944 that one of the most famous dance band leaders, Glenn Miller, visited Britain with his Army Air Force Band. Dance music and dancing certainly didn't win the war, but certainly helped!

People making their way down an air raid shelter shortly after the outbreak of war

Going dancing? Take a gas mask...

Among the immediate casualties of the declaration of war were places of entertainment, which were forced to close. It caused the playwright George Bernard Shaw to write to the newspapers in outraged tones. "May I be allowed to protest vehemently against the order to close all theatres and picture houses during the war? It seems to me a masterstroke of unimaginative stupidity...what agent of Chancellor Hitler is it who suggested that we should all cower in darkness and terror 'for the duration'?"

For most of Britain the duration only lasted until the following Saturday when tens of thousands of people "hungry for entertainment queued up outside Britain's cinemas in the 'safe and 'neutral' areas". The lines were the longest the industry had ever known but there was a new feature outside the cinemas. Large red arrows pointed the direction to the nearest public shelters.

Soon people were back dancing and enjoying London's nightlife, even if it did mean carrying a gas mask and knowing where the nearest public air raid shelter was located.

To begin with the BBC broadcast little but news bulletins, however that quickly changed as there was so little to say. Programming soon returned to normal, which meant that dance records and band shows were once again broadcast.

Coconut Grove

Coconut Grove was in London's Regent Street and just one of the many nightspots that featured a dance band. In its case it was usually a small five or six-piece band. When these photos were taken it was Paul Lombard and his band that were in residence. Before the year was out, George Shearing, then a relatively little-known 21-year-old pianist, and his trio became the house band. Shearing of course went on to find worldwide fame when he moved to America and had a big hit with his composition Lullaby of Birdland about the famous New York club.

These photos were all taken in January 1940 before the Blitz began and shows how life appeared to be going along as normal. This was in the period of 'the phoney war', which came to an end once the Battle of Britain began and the Blitz followed in quick succession. The captions on the original photos name the young ladies and say that they are all 'dance hostesses' and all aged 22!

The conga

Let's dispel one myth. The conga has nothing to do with The Congo in Africa. The truth is the dance originated in Cuba in the 1930s, a time when Havana was the playground of the rich and famous, especially if you were connected in some way to the Mafia and organised crime. It was heady atmosphere in pre-Castro Cuba and it all led to the conga becoming the 'in thing' that quickly spread to America and then across the Atlantic.

Like so many of the dances that have become popular in the latter half of the 20th century it was a street dance. It really took hold when in 1940 it featured in the Hollywood musical film Too Many Girls, in which Desi Arnaz, Lucille Ball's father, appeared as a conga-playing Argentine student; it was popularised by bandleader Xavier Cugat.

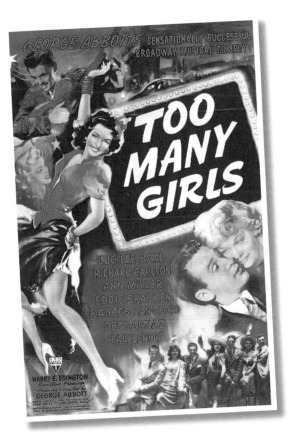

*Bandleader Joe Loss leads a line of people
in a conga at Hammersmith Odeon*

The services' dance instructor

Knowing I was working on this book, a friend of mine came across this at a car boot sale. If this doesn't show you how important dancing was to the war effort I don't know what will!

It looks like it was published in 1941 or 1942 and certainly took the job of teaching servicemen and women how to dance very seriously.

Aside from the normal ballroom dances – the foxtrot, quickstep, waltz and tango – there's information on how to dance the Lambeth Walk and conga.

Left Dancing the samba at the Covent Garden Opera House in London in August 1945

A FEW WORDS OF ADVICE

Be confident but do not become conceited.

Do not dance "affectionately"; it looks detestable to those watching.

Ladies should not leave "make-up" on the man's coat by leaning on him with their heads.

Gentlemen should take care that their shoes are cleaned with something that does not transfer itself on to, and so spoil, the ladies' shoes.

Ladies must not wear narrow skirts, and must not carry bags and other impedimenta while dancing.

Whereas there is no need to dance completely in silence, conversation on the floor should be limited in amount and intensity of sound. It should not become important enough to be the cause of a couple stopping and consequently holding up the traffic, as frequently happens.

Ladies! CARRY YOUR OWN WEIGHT. Do not use the man as a walking arm-chair, and do not clutch at him with your hands, but follow from the hips in the accepted manner.

Endeavour to dance and behave as naturally as possible in the ballroom.

Be polite.

Gentlemen, do not do any complicated movements unless you are sure they are correct and, above all, that you can lead them properly.

Do not assume, if you are a keen dancer, that dancing is the begin-all and end-all of Life; your partner may have accomplishments in another sphere.

PRACTICE, AND STILL PRACTICE, for the time being, at any rate. Ladies, wait for a lead; do not anticipate: it is the worst possible fault.

If you are an acknowledged good dancer, do not be aggressive about it; do not help to maintain that army of "wall-flowers" unless they really deserve it.

32

Danger on the dance floor

The Battle of Britain began on July 10, 1940, and following the Dunkirk evacuation of the BEF in early June there was a distinct shift in the mood of the nation. Dancing was still going on but the threat of potential invasion following the fall of France made everyone more than a little nervous.

A week after the Battle of Britain began it was reported in the Mirror that an 18-year-old dancer was shot in the leg while dancing at the YMCA in Newport, Monmouthshire. Beneath the ballroom was the Boy Scout HQ and a visiting soldier there accidentally discharged his gun and the bullet went through the ceiling and floor, hitting the girl in the leg.

A month later it was reported in the Mirror that any girl serving in the military need not wear her uniform when attending a dance, in order to avoid "wear and tear".

The Luftwaffe's first attack on London was on August 24, 1940, when St Giles Church, Cripplegate, was damaged. The view of the German High Command was that it would break the resolve of the British people if large numbers of civilians were killed. German secret military communiqués, decrypted by the Enigma machine at Bletchley Park, had given the British government cause for great alarm. Messages indicated that the possibility of an invasion was highly likely – indeed 'imminent'. The following night's raids again hit London but, far from breaking the resolve of the British people, life seemed to go on remarkably ordinarily. At one London theatre Ivor Novello entertained the audience by performing Keep The Home Fires Burning after a performance of his musical, I Lived With You. At the Duke of York's theatre the manager offered patrons their money back during a performance of High Temperature after the air raid warning sounded. Nobody left and the show went on

Below Kent residents take part in an impromptu dance while sheltering from attack in a tunnel

Right Dancing in underground tunnels in Chislehurst, Kent, in October 1940, not far from where my mum and dad moved to after the war. They were used as air raid shelters during the Blitz

"THERE WAS A DISTINCT SHIFT IN THE MOOD OF THE NATION. DANCING WAS STILL GOING ON BUT THE THREAT OF POTENTIAL INVASION MADE EVERYONE NERVOUS"

until the end. At others the audience ended up dancing on stage with members of the cast.

By early September the raids had reached a new peak with many civilians being killed. As late summer turned to autumn, and then quickly to winter, the German bombing raids continued to inflict casualties on the civilian population. When I was young, my mum and dad told me about Lord Haw-Haw who broadcast to Britain, taunting us with his absurd claims. His prediction of imminent collapse never came but this, from August 1940, gives you some idea of what he had to say.

"We have learned with horror and disgust that while London was suffering all the nightmares of aerial bombardment a few nights ago, there was a contrast between the situation of the rich and the poor which we

hardly know how to describe. There were two Londons that night. Down by the docks and in the poor districts and the suburbs, people lay dead, or dying in agony from their wounds; but, while their counterparts were suffering only a little distance away, the plutocrats and the favoured lords of creation were making the raid an excuse for their drunken orgies and debaucheries in the saloons of Piccadilly and in the Cafe de Paris.

"Spending on champagne in one night what they would consider enough for a soldier's wife for a month, these monied fools shouted and sang in the streets, crying, as the son of a profiteer baron put it: 'They won't bomb this part of the town! They want the docks! Fill up boys!'."

Above *Dancing around a piano in the East End sometime in 1941. When I see photos like this it reminds me why I love Londoners so much and the spirit of my family that was not crushed by Hitler during the Second World War*

Inset *Sailors dancing to a military band on the Hoe in Plymouth 1941*

Opposite *Women ambulance drivers have a dance in 1939*

Tragedy at the Café de Paris

The dangers of the Blitz for people out enjoying themselves were nowhere better illustrated than when London's Café de Paris was bombed in March 1941.

The Mirror reported the events but for censorship reasons did not reveal the exact location.

A packed dance hall was wrecked, and a bus and a row of shops and offices were demolished when bombs fell in a London area on Saturday night.

Several people in the dance hall were killed, and others were injured and died in hospital. At least half the people in the fully occupied bus, and people sheltering in neighbouring doorways, were killed. Sixty couples – munitions workers, soldiers on leave and typists – were on the dance floor when four H.E. bombs whistled down.

One hit the dance hall, blowing out one end of it.

> **"THE LIGHTS CRASHED DOWN. DANCERS WERE FLUNG TO THE FLOOR. DEBRIS CASCADED ON YOUNG COUPLES"**

Right Clearly visible in the aftermath of the bombing is Joey Deniz's guitar; the West Indian guitarist who, although injured, survived the blast

Left The entrance to Café de Paris in November 1950, two years after it reopened. Commissionaires and doormen in pukka uniforms is another thing you don't see these days

Below right Formation dancers at the Café de Paris in 1957

The lights crashed down. Dancers were flung to the floor. Debris cascaded on young couples.

In actual fact 30 people died and around 60 were injured at the Café de Paris on a night when London Civil Defence records show that 159 people were killed and 338 seriously injured in 238 separate incidents.

Among the dead was the West Indian bandleader Ken 'Snakehips' Johnson. Johnson had no signs of injury, he had a flower in his buttonhole and was 26 years old.

After I took up ballroom dancing I danced there many times and it was later that I found out the story of the tragedy.

The Café De Paris, close to London's Leicester Square, opened in 1924 and by the 1930s was a fashionable nightclub frequented by the rich and famous, and even the Prince of Wales was a regular visitor.

During the war the club was packed most nights of the week and despite air raid warnings the band just kept on playing, but not this time.

➤

This tragedy encouraged one woman to write to the paper condemning what went on. Fortunately, it was not a sentiment shared by everyone.

"I have long felt that it is a disgrace to what we call our 'War Effort' that people should fritter their time away dancing night after night. The recent destruction of two dance halls seems like a Divine Judgment on the subject.

"After all, who can call dancing a 'healthy' recreation? Young men and women herded together, in a stuffy atmosphere, in close proximity to one another, is hardly conducive to the moral wellbeing of the race. I read that the Minister of Home Security is considering closing all dance halls during air raids. So far, so good. I would go further and urge him to shut them after blackout time, anyway.

"The spare time of all of us . . . soldiers, sailors, airmen, men and women workers is better spent in healthful sleep or exercise than in flaunting around these haunts."
"WOMAN WAR WORKER" of Huddersfield.

The loss of life in the Café de Paris tragedy was small compared to the 73 people, including soldiers and airmen, that were killed at the Palace Dance Hall in Putney in November 1943. With fewer raids taking place by this time people were much less concerned about seeking the safety of a shelter. People just kept on dancing even though the air raid warning had sounded.

*All that remained of the Palace Dance Hall in Putney High Street and,
left, the victims' clothing piled up next to the destroyed building*

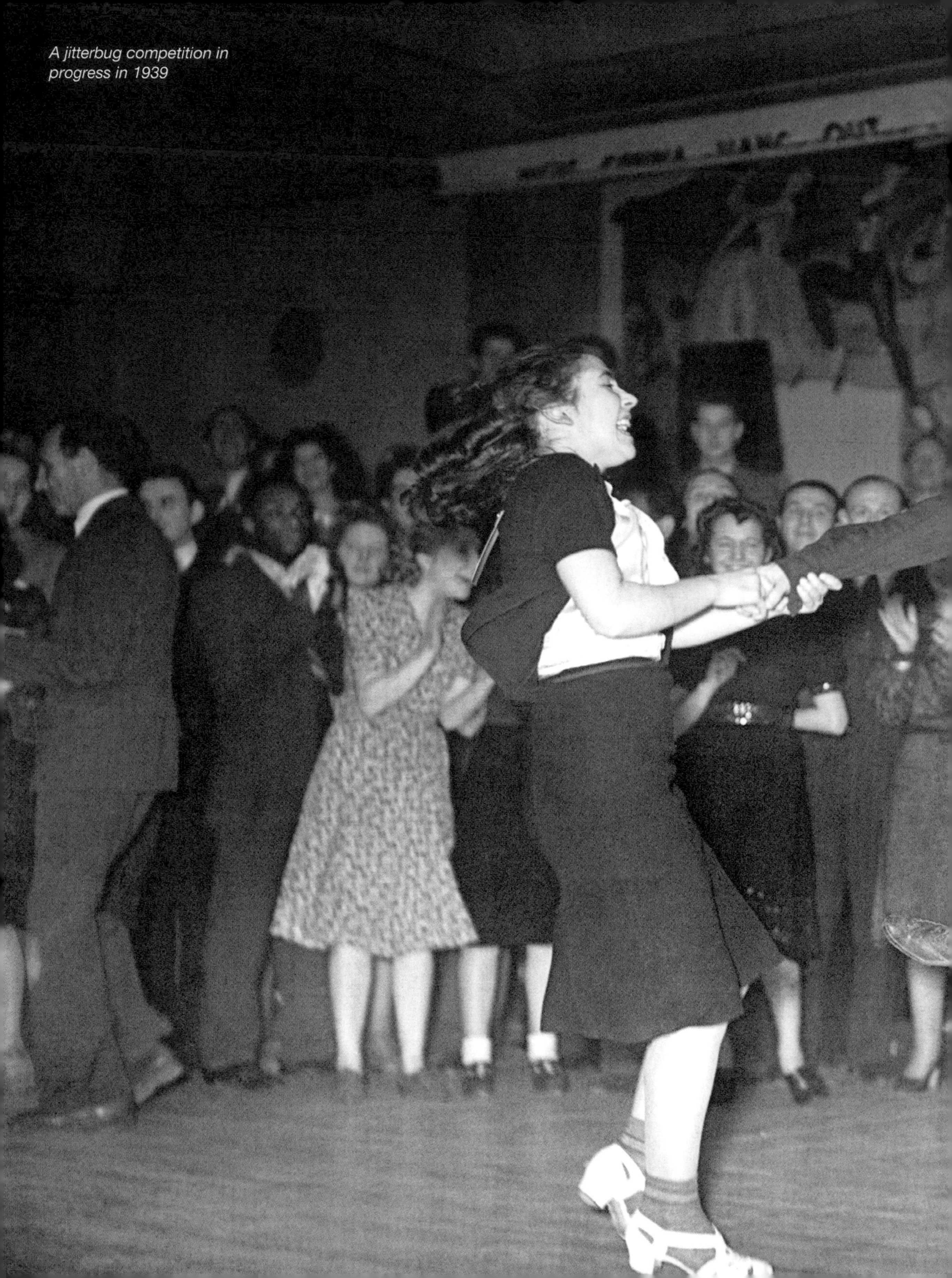

A jitterbug competition in progress in 1939

THE ST. JOHN AMBULANCE BRIGADE
(Millom Division).

This is to Certify

That *Mrs. L. G. Goodman*
of Lincoln Street, Millom, Cumb
was adjudged the winner
of the S.C. Ballroom Champ-
ionship. Donald Ross. Hon. Sec.

Date *17.10.41.*

Above *Young boys choosing their ballroom dancing partners near Hindhead, Surrey, in May 1941*

Left *My mum won a St John's Ambulance Dancing championship in October 1941*

Above right *Couples dancing at a work party at a factory in a northern industrial city in October 1942*

Right *Gunner John Hiller and fiancé Miss Trinder buy an engagement ring at a jewelers in London. They, like so many couples during this era, met at a dance*

Far right *Children dance to the sound of a barrel organ in one of London's bombed streets on February 5, 1941*

Tough life for fun-loving Land Girls

By the late summer of 1940 nearly 50,000 men had been 'lost to the land' through enlistment or switching to better-paid work in towns and cities.

The Women's Land Army had first been set up in the First World War but was resurrected in 1939 in anticipation of a shortfall in manpower.

By August 1940 all the places in the Women's Land Army were filled.

While the average farm worker earned 38 shillings a week, which in itself was about half the national average wage, Land Girls were paid 28 shillings a week; of this around half paid for board and lodgings.

There were also no set holiday entitlements and while many of the girls lived in hostels, some of which were vacant country houses, and had a good deal of fun there was no getting away from the fact that it was back-breaking work involving long hours especially in the long days of summer.

Below Women munitions workers dance the jitterbug at a tea dance in April 1943

Right Women's Land Army girls at Leamington Spa kicking the old year out and welcoming in the new in January 1943

The Columbia Club (American Red Cross Club) organised a hayride and picnic lunch for the US forces and their friends as a celebration of American Independence Day. A soldier and his girlfriend are pictured doing the jitterbug on July 4, 1943

"WHILE MANY OF
THE GIRLS LIVED
IN HOSTELS, SOME
OF WHICH WERE
VACANT COUNTRY
HOUSES, AND HAD
A GOOD DEAL OF
FUN THERE WAS NO
GETTING AWAY FROM
THE FACT IT WAS
BACK-BREAKING
WORK"

Above Members of the Auxiliary Territorial
Service learn some moves shortly before being
demobbed

Left Dancing time at a Land Army holiday camp
at Cookham in October 1943

A scene from the film Sun Valley Serenade

Mystery death of big band legend

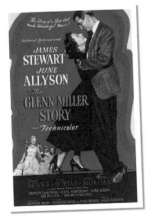

Glenn Miller, for many people, is big band dance music. His sweet sound was popular in the UK throughout the war, particularly so because Captain Glenn Miller's Army Air Force Band visited Britain and toured extensively. He was heard on the radio playing live as well as on his numerous record releases.

Born in 1904, Miller learned to play trombone and after dropping out of college he joined a number of big bands in the 1920s, and by the early 1930s was both playing with and arranging for the Dorsey Brother's Orchestra. By 1938 he was leading his own orchestra and recording. Come 1939 he was just about the most popular orchestra in America and before long he started having hit records including In the Mood, American Patrol, Chattanooga Choo Choo, Tuxedo Junction,

Moonlight Serenade, Little Brown Jug and Pennsylvania 6-5000. In February 1942 Glenn Miller was awarded the first Gold Disc for sales of over one million of a recording. Chattanooga Choo Choo had made No.1 on the American charts for nine weeks at the end of 1941 and was also a big seller in Britain

In 1941 he appeared in the film Sun Valley Serenade and in 1942 his band were featured in Orchestra Wives, which all added to Miller's fame.

It was in 1942 that he joined up and became Captain Glenn Miller in charge of the Army Air Force Band. In 1944 they travelled to Britain where they gave hundreds of performances. On December 15, 1944, Miller was flying from the United Kingdom to Paris when his aircraft mysteriously disappeared over the English Channel. Neither the aircraft, nor his remains have ever been found. It's led to many different theories including some that trawl the realms of conspiracy, including one that suggests he was on a spying mission. Whatever the truth there's no denying the fact that his legend lives on through his music and he remains the most popular big band leader of all time.

SONGS
THAT GOT BRITAIN
DANCING

In The Mood

It's probably one of the most iconic opening few bars of any dance band era recording and was a chart-topping record in America and also very popular during the war in Britain.

Its popularity stems from it being featured in the film Sun Valley Serenade that starred Sonje Henie and John Payne.

In The Mood was written by Joe Garland and Andy Razaf, the latter famous for his work with the brilliant Fats Waller, and the two of them based their composition on a tune called Tar Paper Stomp by trumpeter Wingy Manone; the riff was also used in a tune called 'Hot and Anxious,' recorded by Fletcher Henderson Orchestra.

Neither tune had been written down, and so it was not copyrighted, which is what allowed Razaf and Garland to claim the copyright.

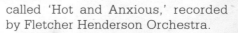

Dance bands swing into action

While I was looking into the role of dance bands during the war a friend of mine sent me a cutting from the Melody Maker dated May 1941. It's a great reflection on just what everyone thought about music and dancing in the Second World War. The Melody Maker story was aimed at winning the hearts and minds of German airmen. According to the report in the newspaper for musicians and fans of popular music, the BBC planned a 'Radio Dance Music Blitz on Germany'.

Every afternoon at 4 p.m., on 373 metres, a new form of blitzkrieg descends on Germany. But it's not the RAF, which delivers it this time, only the best dance orchestras in Britain, presented with the acme of showmanship. Wednesdays are the high spot.

For then the programme is specially presented for the entertainment of the German Luftwaffe and on several occasions bands composed of RAF players have actually broadcast to their German counterparts! A week ago an RAF band with some famous players included in the personnel aired

RADIO DANCE MUSIC BLITZ ON GERMANY!

on this programme, and the show they gave has already resulted in a surprisingly large number of letters from listeners, all over the world – and some of them from Germany. For the daily airings Geraldo has become almost the house band, although Ambrose, Mantovani and Jack Payne have already broadcast in the series. On Wednesdays it is the BBC policy to include as many of the RAF combinations as possible.

The entertainment angle in these programmes is definitely swing, with only a small proportion of sweet tunes thrown in to make up the balance. The success of the Wednesday afternoons has caused the BBC seriously to consider two special Luftwaffe airings each week, and a neutral journalist who recently arrived in this country after touring Germany and occupied France is said to have told the officials of the corporation that he actually heard the programme being received in the officers'

mess at a German aerodrome! Too much credit has been given to Dr. Joe Goebbels for his propaganda. We, for our part, tip our hats to the BBC for its realisation of the persuasive powers of really good dance music put over with imagination and skill for the cause of Britain.

Opposite *Three sax players from the ATS dance band are seen here performing in January 1944*

Below *The ATS dance band with their conductor, Junior Commander Angela Stebbings, at a rehearsal in January 1944*

Peace in Europe as Nazis surrender

On Monday, May 7, at around 4.30pm, news came in from General Eisenhower's HQ that the terms of the Nazi surrender had been negotiated and settled. Later that evening on the BBC news it was announced that the following day would be a holiday.

"This is the BBC Home Service. We are interrupting programmes to make the following announcement. It is understood that in accordance with arrangements between the three great powers an official announcement will be broadcast by the Prime Minister at 3 o'clock tomorrow, Tuesday afternoon, the 8th of May.

"In view of this fact tomorrow, Tuesday, will be treated as Victory in Europe Day and will be regarded as a holiday. The day following, Wednesday, the 9th of May, will also be a holiday. His Majesty the King will broadcast to the people of the British Empire and Commonwealth tomorrow at 9pm British double summer time."

John Snagge, 7.45pm, May 7, 1945

Above Lyceum Theatre opens as a dance hall – the old boxes now used to watch the dancers and the band

Right Dancing in a London street on VE Day, the end of the war in Europe in 1945

People queing for admittance at the Lyceum Theatre despite it being packed inside on October 22, 1945

Above Bill Pethers and his Orchestra performing outside the Coventry Hippodrome Theatre on VE Day evening, May 8, 1945

Opposite I just had to share this photo with you. It's Bruce Forsyth playing his ukulele in 1945 aged seventeen. Not strictly dancing, but as Brucie would say, 'keep dancing'

"NEWS CAME THROUGH FROM GENERAL EISENHOWER'S HQ THAT THE TERMS OF THE NAZI SURRENDER HAD BEEN NEGOTIATED AND SETTLED"

Dancing in the ballroom at the
Butlin's holiday camp in Skegness

Holiday camps swept us all off our feet

Back in the 1950s and 1960s holiday camps played a huge part in the ballroom and Latin American dancing scene. It was not just because Pontins and Butlin's sponsored competitions but also because tens of thousands of British holidaymakers danced their feet off night after night at their huge camps. Butlin's camps at Clacton and Ayr could each take 2,500 a week, while Skegness, Pwllheli and Filey could take a massive 5,500 visitors.

In need of a dance partner...

I started going to the Erith Dance Studio more regularly than ever but soon there was a problem – I didn't have a partner as my girlfriend and me had split up after a rather disastrous package holiday in Spain; some contretemps with a Spanish waiter. The big problem I had was I was about to take my bronze medal for ballroom dancing and without a partner that's a bit tricky.

To the rescue came Miss Tolhurst, who owned the studio with her husband; they suggested dancing with their daughter Cherry, who naturally given her parents' talent was a very good dancer.

Cherry had done all her medals, she was a really accomplished and lovely dancer, and so it made me look so much better. In the run-up to the medal examination Henry Kingston, Joy Tolurst's husband, began to take a keen interest in what we were doing.

On the day of the medal test Henry stood and watched,

Bottom Butlin's holiday camp, October 1961

Below Sir Billy Butlin in 1962 at his Minehead holiday camp

Right Butlin's Holiday Camp Dance at Empress Stadium, Earls Court, in 1939

"THE BIG PROBLEM I HAD WAS THAT I WAS ABOUT TO TAKE MY BRONZE MEDAL FOR BALLROOM DANCING AND WITHOUT A PARTNER THAT'S A BIT TRICKY"

and afterwards he said to me, "I've watched you dancing with my daughter and I think you have the potential to become quite a good dancer…if you work at it. Would you like to continue dancing with Cherry and I will give you private tuition? You can see how you get on; needless to say there will be no charge. She has never had any interest in dancing competitively, but you've changed all that Len."

"That would be great Mr Kingston."

Cherry must have told her dad that she enjoyed dancing with me but I wasn't at all sure what 'dancing competitively' really meant. I was soon to find out and my life would change forever.

It was an incredible experience being coached by Cherry's father, although to begin with it was just the waltz and the quickstep. His teaching methods were rigorous and centred upon the fact that it was vital to perfect each and every dance, to have it so ingrained ➤

upon your brain that you never ever lose the technique.

Even today I can look at dancers and instinctively know something is wrong, it's not something I'm even aware of doing. I can look at a couple's heads and I know there's something not right with their feet. I learnt this from Henry Kingston's coaching, he taught me a lot about the technique and the kinetics of movement. We began learning new dances and during the summer Henry told us he felt we were ready to enter our first competition, where else but Pontins holiday camps.

The camps had been started by Fred Pontin in the late 1940s to give people an affordable place to go on holiday at the seaside in Britain. They not only offered accommodation but there was also an extensive programme of nightly entertainment of all different kinds, although the emphasis was very much on family

> "EVEN TODAY I CAN LOOK AT DANCERS AND INSTINCTIVELY KNOW THAT SOMETHING IS WRONG"

Above *Contestants in the Miss Lovely Legs competition in 1954, a bit before my time at Pontins but it was something that was no different even a decade or so later*

fun – it was all very Hi-De-Hi.

During the season, at every one of their thirty camps, Pontins ran competitions; including darts, Miss Lovely Legs, the Most Eligible Escort, Miss Pontin, singing contests and, not surprisingly, dancing. If you won through the various rounds you eventually ended up at the final at the Royal Albert Hall.

It meant that we would have to spend a week at a Pontins holiday camp. At the end of the season one of their camps was designated as the 'host camp' for the dancers and so the winners from all thirty camps throughout the summer would go there for the first phase of the dance-off. Our competition camp was Camber Sands in Kent.

After a disaster in me getting kitted out in white tie and tails we eventually pitched up at Pontins and we won! When we did our waltz and quickstep all the holidaymakers stood up and clapped. It was the first time I'd ever been applauded for my dancing and I was really chuffed.

After Camber Sands we headed to Osmington Bay, near Weymouth in Dorset, for the next round. We won again! This meant we were in the final at the Royal Albert Hall dancing to Joe Loss and his orchestra. There were twelve couples, we got down to the last six and then, almost unbelievably, we won.

Fred Pontin himself presented us with our prize and we had our picture taken with him and Henry Kingston. The fact is that Henry was held in awe by many of the professional judges so it was no wonder they took notice of us. I learned a lot from my first competition. Ballroom dancing is much like a sport; dedication, training, fitness and a strong work ethic all come into play; if you really want to progress to a high level it'll never happen without a huge amount of effort.

March Of The Mods

I was a Mod! Mainly because I liked the clothes. Being a Mod was truly great from Easter to August bank holiday; most Saturday mornings we left Kent for our base at the Skylark, a pub just off Brighton beach. Up the road from Black Rock was the Fortune of War, which was the Rockers pub – we had our pub and they had their pub. It was in the Skylark that I first heard the Beatles on their jukebox; it

stopped me in my tracks. From that day on I became a fan although I never did get to see them. I'd seen Buddy Holly at the Granada Woolwich, Ray Charles at the Gaumont Lewisham, Cliff Richard and Marti Wilde at the Granada Dartford – but never the Beatles.

Dancing to Joe Loss's orchestra at the Royal Albert Hall was the icing on the cake, not that he played his recording March Of The Mods. It is one of those records that everyone of a certain age knows, but it was surprisingly not such a big hit, only ever reaching No.31 on the charts in late 1964/early 1965.

Joe Loss came from Spitalfields, not far from me, and a place I would go with my grandad on his barrow to buy fruit and veg in the late 1940s and early 1950s. Loss had been leading bands since the 1930s and in the early 1960s he had a number of other hits that were all records to dance to. These included Wheels-Cha Cha and Must Be Madison. The Madison originated in Columbus, Ohio, and is a line dance that features a regular back-and-forth pattern interspersed with 'called' steps.

March Of The Mods (Finnjenka Dance) was also a novelty dance, a lot like the Lambeth Walk but based on a Finnish dance. It involves a lot of hopping and stepping and to be honest it doesn't take a lot of skill, everyone can do it…and that's the point, from kids to grannies at parties, all did the March Of The Mods.

Above Mods on the beach in Brighton August 1964; I'm pretty certain I'm not in the photo!

Right Mods rounded up after clashes with Rockers at Brighton in April 1965

Above Mods' scooters lined up in Brighton, August 1964

Right I never did fancy the way Rockers dressed or danced!

Below right The Bishop of Southwark with a group of Hells Angels in the local pub, The Bell, in Sydenham, Kent, in 1970

Below Mods on their scooters seen here leaving Clacton at the end of the bank holiday weekend. Over the 1964 Easter weekend several scuffles between Mods and Rockers broke out in the Essex seaside town

Taking next step

The next step forward in our competitive career was with the competition, Butlin's holiday camps. This one was called Dancing Stars Of Tomorrow. It was another for novice dancers on the first rung of competition dancing but a step up from Pontins. There was another problem; it was not just the waltz and the quickstep, this time we had to dance the cha cha cha, a whole new learning experience.

Henry didn't teach Latin dancing so we went to a lady called Nina Hunt whose dance studio was in Balham. It's strange but in the late 1960s and 1970s most of the top ballroom and Latin teachers were based in South London. There were Bill and Bobbie Irvine, Walter Laird, Len Scrivener, Sonny Binick and Wally Fryer, a near endless list of former champions.

To understand how good a teacher Nina Hunt was it was a bit like sending someone that had never played golf, other than pitch and putt, for a private

Above *That's me, aged 22, in 1966. We came third in the Kent Championships, the bad news was there were only three contestants*

Below *Kids in the Vienna Ballroom at Butlin's in Filey, North Yorkshire, in the 1950s. It gives you an idea of the size of these places – they looked so swish back in the day*

People of all ages enjoyed themselves at Butlin's, as this picture taken in the 1940s shows

"WE DANCED VERY BADLY IN THE FIRST ROUND – SOME OF MY WORKMATES HECKLED ME!"

lesson with Tiger Woods! After what seemed like endless hours of teaching and practice it was time for the competition itself that was to again be held at the Royal Albert Hall. We danced very badly in the first round and Henry was not happy with us; it was partly down to some of my workmates from the docks heckling me!

Much to my surprise, we got through to the second round, and thankfully my nerves had subsided somewhat. This round was made up of 24 dancers and we danced much better and got through to round three – the last twelve. We made it into the

➤

final along with five other couples. There were two from Scotland, one from Northern Ireland and three from England, including Cherry and myself.

After we danced in the final we got a standing ovation from my workmates but they were not the judges! "In first place number four." It was one of the Scottish couples. Next up it was 24, then 31 – we hadn't made the top three. At that point another feeling kicked in. Please don't let us be last!

"In fourth place, couple number 36, Mr Len Goodman and Miss Cherry Kingston."

In that moment my feeling of invincibility was shattered forever. I realised then, and it's a feeling that's never left me, that it's hard work that makes winners. It has of course got something to do with talent, there's also a little bit of luck that comes into play, but as the old saying goes – the harder I work, the luckier I become.

"I REALISED THEN THAT IT'S HARD WORK THAT MAKES WINNERS"

Above *The ballroom at Butlin's Barry Island where I danced on a number of occasions*

Opposite *In action on the dance floor with Cherry Kingston*

The New Bedford Picture House, in Eglinton Street, Glasgow, pictured on December 23, 1932, a week before it opened. Somehow this seems to conjure up the magic of the movies and what excited us so much about "going to the pictures"

CHAPTER 5

Dancing on the silver screen

The films of Fred Astaire and Ginger Rogers encouraged more people to go dancing in ballrooms during the 1930s than anything else. The music they danced to was added to the set lists of all the dance bands of the day. With movies becoming ever more colourful and inventive, dance featured in many of them, creating popular dance crazes and reflecting them. When the heyday of Hollywood musicals waned in the 1950s some may have thought we would never see dancing in films in quite the same way ever again. In some ways we didn't but, ever since, there have been dance film scenes that have excited and inspired us.

They can talk, sing... and dance!

When The Jazz Singer came out in 1927 it revolutionised the movies; it was the first film to feature synchronised talking. The era of the talkies began and not unnaturally it was musicals that captured the imagination of moviegoers everywhere. Prior to The Jazz Singer, which starred Al Jolson, films had featured dancers but they were always accompanied at a cinema with musicians, often a lone pianist, playing along to provide the soundtrack, fine if the musicians were able to synchronise their playing, but all too often it was out of sync.

In the immediate aftermath of The Jazz Singer there was a plethora of movies that featured singing and dancing – more than 60 in 1929 and 80 in 1930. One of the first films to catch the public imagination to feature dancing was the 1929 film The Gold Diggers of Broadway, which was the second all-talking feature length film – it was also a remake of a silent film.

It featured some lavish dance scenes and starred Ann Pennington, 'the astounding dancing of Ann Pennington' as it said on the advertising for the film. Lavish set pieces with dancers were just the kind of thing that movie audiences lapped up, particularly because at this time few people could see this kind of thing live on stage. The closing sequence featuring men in top hats and tails with beautifully dressed women in an incredible tap dance routine became something of a template for musicals in the next decade. It was pure Hollywood!

Also in 1929 there was On With The Show, which again was in colour and featured singing and lavish dance numbers. It also starred Ethel Waters, one of the first black artists to make an impact in Hollywood.

Another favourite of mine is The Show Of Shows that featured a fantastic finale with the song Lady Luck and a cast of maybe a hundred dancers in a full-on display of fabulous dancing.

Now, as you can imagine, even I'm not old enough to have seen all these films at the time, nor did I see all of them on TV as so many of the movies from this era have been lost.

Thankfully, snippets have survived and short clips can be seen on YouTube. It really is a marvellous thing that this dancing history has not been totally lost. If you have the internet you can spend many a wet Sunday afternoon watching some fabulous features.

"IN THE IMMEDIATE AFTERMATH OF THE JAZZ SINGER THERE WAS A PLETHORA OF MOVIES THAT FEATURED SINGING AND DANCING "

Al Jolson, with his wife Ruby in 1928, a year after The Jazz Singer was released

Busby Berkeley's golden touch

From the dizzy heights of 1930, the number of musicals released during the following year plummeted to under a dozen, and it may well have declined even more but for the genius of one man – Busby Berkeley.

He was hired by MGM in 1930 and while his first film Whoopee! had few of the trademark BB touches that we have come to love, it did point the way to where his fertile imagination was leading. Over the following few years he began to develop his skills for staging amazing set piece routines with dancers – and lots of them.

In 1933 he directed the choreography in 42nd Street and it was totally amazing. It was Ruby Keeler's first film and the climax features her singing and dancing the title song before being joined, so it seems, by every dancer in Hollywood. Unmissable!

42nd Street was revived as a stage musical on Broadway and the West End and this is what many people have seen. In fact the stage musical also incorporates numbers from another one of Berkeley's big successes, The Gold Diggers Of 1933, most notably We're In The Money, that is sung by 21-year-old Ginger Rogers. The sequence is wonderful, with showgirls dancing with huge coins. It is one of Hollywood's great dance moments. If you think this is amazing the Shadow Waltz sequence is astonishing; almost impossible to imagine someone coming up with such an innovative idea; it features neon violins danced into amazing shapes. Apparently, Berkeley got the idea for from a vaudeville act he once saw – he added the neon on the violins as an afterthought.

Two years later, Berkeley directed The Gold Diggers Of 1935 that includes The Lullaby Of Broadway that was

"THE SEQUENCE IS WONDERFUL, WITH SHOWGIRLS DANCING WITH HUGE COINS. IT IS ONE OF HOLLYWOOD'S GREAT DANCE MOMENTS"

A scene from 42nd Street. Hollywood provided work for thousands of dancers

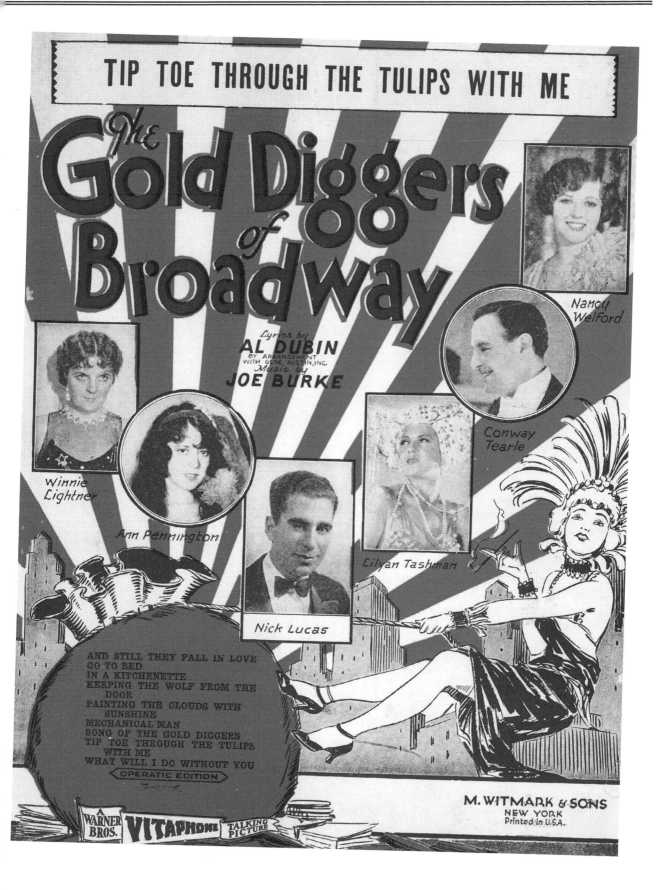

➤ also used in the stage adaptation of 42nd Street. Lullaby Of Broadway is another unforgettable Berkeley dance routine. Sung by Wini Shaw, it then morphs into an incredible routine that is pure joy for tap-dancing fans. Berkeley, the son of an actress, directed numerous Hollywood movies in the 1930s and choreographed many of them as well. His other memorable movie moments include I Got Rhythm starring Judy Garland in Girl Crazy (1943) and Carmen Miranda's The Lady In The Tutti-Frutti Hat from The Gang's All Here, also in 1943. Berkeley had worked with Judy Garland on The Wizard Of Oz on which he choreographed a sequence for the scarecrow, If I Only Had A Brain, that was eventually dropped from the film but can be seen on YouTube.

What makes Busby Berkeley so important? Well, there is not a choreographer that has not borrowed or been inspired in some way or another by his fertile imagination and the sheer audacity of his dance routines.

While I saw many of these classic movies on the TV over the years I've also gone back to check them out on YouTube. If those old Busby Berkeley films don't make you want to dance I don't know what will.

Top left and above *More scenes from the classic Hollywood musical 42nd Street*

Top right *Judy Garland, star of The Wizard Of Oz and Girl Crazy*

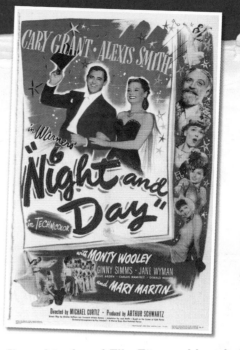

Night And Day

This is one of those beautiful songs that is perfect for slow dancing. It was originally written by Cole Porter for the stage play Gay Divorce and almost immediately it became popular on both sides of the Atlantic when Fred Astaire recorded it.

While it has a lovely melody, it is the sentiment of lyric that resonated with so many people, "Night and day, you are the one."

What more could anyone ask from their loved one? While there were no proper music charts back in the 1930s it became the biggest-selling song of the year and its popularity increased still further when Astaire recorded it again in 1934 for the film version of the play. I remember seeing Spike Milligan on Breakfast With Frost complaining about modern music, saying, "All these kids have never heard a tune like Night And Day'" – he's right!

Porter himself claimed on a number of occasions that the Islamic call to worship he heard on a trip to Morocco influenced his writing. The American Society of Composers, Authors and Publishers list Night And Day as one of its most recorded songs of the 20th century and people are still recording it today.

One of those who has recorded it more than most is Frank Sinatra, firstly in 1942 with Axel Stordahl in his first solo session. In fact he did it five times on separate releases, perhaps most memorably with Nelson Riddle in 1956 for the album A Swingin' Affair!. He even did a disco version in 1977 but I would avoid that one.

I'm a big fan of Ella Fitzgerald and she recorded a wonderful version of Night And Day. She recorded it at Capitol Records studio in Los Angeles, the same studio in which Frank Sinatra recorded all his classic albums.

It was for the album, Ella Fitzgerald Sings The Cole Porter Songbook. It is essential listening, a record that no self-respecting lover of music should live without this wonderful music. There's a song Reminiscing by an Australian group called The Little River Band. In it they sing, "And the Porter tune, made us dance across the room" – they were not wrong!

Jazz singer Ella Fitzgerald recorded a wonderful version of Night And Day

Dancing gods of the silver screen

Fred and Ginger, Rogers and Astaire, no matter which way round it goes or how you say it, you're talking about two of the silver screen's dancing gods! When they burst onto the cinema screens in 1933 in the film Flying Down To Rio they were an instantaneous hit with moviegoers…and they quickly became, and have remained, an inspiration to just about anyone who loves to dance.

It was Ginger Rogers who first appeared on celluloid, in a movie short in 1929 before her appearances in 42nd Street and Gold Diggers Of 1933. This was the same year that Astaire made his debut when he had a small part in a Clark Gable and Joan Crawford film called Dancing Lady.

Born Frederick Austerlitz, he was relatively old at 33 when his movie career began. He had started out in Vaudeville with his sister, Adele, and they got their break on Broadway in 1917. During the 1920s, Fred and Adele appeared on both Broadway and on the London stage in shows that included George and Ira Gershwin's Lady Be Good (1924) and Funny Face (1927), and later in The Band Wagon (1931). Fred's tap-dancing was the best, as one critic wrote in 1930, "I don't think that I will plunge the nation into war by stating that Fred is the greatest tap-dancer in the world." Fred and Adele's professional partnership ended when she married the second son of the Duke of Devonshire; her brother carried on alone, starring in Gay Divorce in both London and Broadway.

I found the review of Fred's performance in the Daily Mirror the day after Gay Divorce opened in London on November 2, 1933.

"His dancing has a sort of humorous eloquence. It is full of surprises. Always it has the charm of appearing to be spontaneous. Claire Luce makes him a good partner. The two of them have a big number at the end of the second act. It is called Night And Day, an insinuating melody against a rhythmic background and is going to be the 'nuisance' of the winter season."

By "nuisance" I take it the reviewer means a hit – he certainly had that right!

➤

Top left *Fred Astaire attending the Royal Command Performance in November 1965*

Above *Ginger Rogers with husband Jacques Bergerac in the film Lifetime in January 1954*

Left *Ginger Roger signing autographs at the Cannes Film Festival in 1960 with fellow actress Kim Novak*

"FRED AND GINGER, ROGERS AND ASTAIRE, NO MATTER WHICH WAY ROUND IT GOES OR HOW YOU SAY IT, YOU'RE TALKING ABOUT TWO OF THE SILVER SCREEN'S DANCING GODS!"

THEY'RE DANCING CHEEK-TO-CHEEK AGAIN!

"TOP HAT IN 1935 FEATURES FRED'S MOST AMAZING TAP ROUTINE TO TOP HAT, WHITE TIE AND TAILS"

Ginger Rogers was born Virginia Katherine McMath in 1911 and got the name 'Ginger' because her young cousin struggled to pronounce Virginia and could only manage 'Ginga'.

She won a Charleston dancing contest at 15 and went on tour for six months and at 17 Ginger married Jack Culpepper, a vaudeville artist, and they briefly performed as 'Ginger and Pepper'. The marriage was over very quickly and Ginger went back on the road ending up in New York City, where she got work singing on the radio before making her Broadway debut in a musical called Top Speed, which opened at Christmas Day 1929.

Two weeks later, Rogers was chosen to star on Broadway in the Gershwins' Girl Crazy; Fred Astaire helped the dancers with their choreography. Her movie debut soon followed and she quickly got bigger parts in Hollywood – the camera loved her. Fred and Ginger filmed Flying Down To Rio before Astaire came to London to star in Gay Divorce.

He probably had no idea just how popular their movie would be when it was released just after Christmas 1933.

In fact Fred and Ginger were not the leads in the film, that honour went to Delores del Rio and Gene Raymond. The film is the usual Hollywood fare but includes the great sequence where Fred sings and dances the film's title song at the hotel while the girls dance on the wings of the aircraft that fly overhead. The first time that the real Astaire, Rogers magic was ever seen on screen was when they danced the carioca. There is a fabulous moment about a minute and a half into the sequence

Ginger Rogers during a visit to Britain in 1955

FRED ASTAIRE GINGER ROGERS

IN THE SUPER-DREADNAUGHT OF MUSICAL SHOWS

FOLLOW THE FLEET

RANDOLPH SCOTT
HARRIET HILLIARD
ASTRID ALLWYN

LYRICS AND MUSIC BY IRVING BERLIN

DIRECTED BY MARK SANDRICH · A PANDRO S. BERMAN PRODUCTION

when they touch foreheads and smile at one another. It's as though they knew at that instant that they had a very special chemistry.

So special was that chemistry that as soon as Fred finished his run in London he headed to Hollywood to film the first of nine musicals that he and Ginger made together during the 1930s.

The first was The Gay Divorcee, the stage production renamed, and it opened in October 1934 with Fred and Ginger this time getting star billing as 'The King and Queen of the Carioca'.

The film features The Continental, which won the very first Academy Award for Best Original Song in a movie.

Of course The Gay Divorcee also features Night And Day, which Fred sings to Ginger in a hotel room overlooking the English Channel. It's another one of those movie moments that have you believing in true romance and when they dance together they define the elegance of ballroom dancing like no-one else. They make everything look so effortless, but it's the kind of effortlessness that can only come from practice coupled with natural talent.

I love the moment when they finish and Fred says, "cigarette". Ginger gives him the most amazing look and just softly shakes her head. There followed a string of classic movies starting with Roberta in 1935 that includes I'll Be Hard To Handle, where Astaire and Rogers tap dance and "talk with their feet," and I Won't Dance, which is sung by Ginger and followed by a solo dance by Fred.

Top Hat in 1935 features Fred's most amazing tap routine to Top Hat, White Tie And Tails.

There's also Fred and Ginger dancing to Isn't This A Lovely Day (To Be Caught In The Rain), but for many the highlight is them dancing to Cheek To Cheek; it's another one of those romantic movie dance moments that can hardly be bettered.

Follow The Fleet from 1936 features another classic dance duet, this time Let's Face The Music And Dance. Fred starts out singing the song to Ginger before they begin their dance together. The dance sequence was filmed in one continuous

➤

➤ take lasting almost three minutes and during the first take, the sleeves of Ginger's dress, which was heavily weighted to make them elegantly swirl, hit Fred Astaire in the face.

Though its barely discernible the director decided to keep this take rather than any of the twenty other takes they did. Considered by many to be their best musical together, Swing Time from 1936 includes the Never Gonna Dance sequence which begins to the music of The Way You Look Tonight.

At the start of the routine Fred and Ginger are just walking around the dance floor together, no-one has ever walked more gracefully than they do.

There's also Bojangles Of Harlem which is Fred solo-tapping in the style of the great Bill 'Bojangles' Robinson. Astaire is dressed in the style of the character Sportin' Life that Astaire's one-time dance teacher John W. Bubbles played the year before in the Gershwins' Porgy And Bess.

Carefree in 1938 has only one memorable song in it, Change Partners, written by Irving Berlin, but it has some great dancing with many more lifts in it than on earlier films. The lifts were there because they were preparing for the film The Story Of Vernon and Irene Castle that was released in 1939.

It tells the true story of an American dancer Irene Foote who managed to convince the British vaudeville comic Vernon Castle to give up slapstick comedy and concentrate on ballroom dancing. There are many things that make these films so memorable, but from a dancer's standpoint there is one special thing that Astaire did that makes them so brilliant. He insisted that the camera remain still and film his and Ginger's dance routines in a single shot, keeping the ➤

Opposite *The Band Wagon starring Fred Astaire and Cyd Charisse*

"HE INSISTED THAT THE CAMERA REMAIN STILL AND FILM HIS AND GINGER'S DANCE ROUTINES IN A SINGLE SHOT"

➤ dancers in full view at all times. Because of this we can study them so well, see so clearly how they dance, the little subtle things that they do and most importantly to learn from them. Both of the last two films that Fred and Ginger made for RKO Pictures were box office flops, mainly down to the cost of production, but also probably because their partnership and style of films had run their course with the public.

Astaire himself was labelled "box office poison" by one magazine. In 1940 he made The Broadway Melody of 1940 with the brilliant tap-dancer, Eleanor Powell, in which they danced together to Cole Porter's Begin The Beguine. He starred with Bing Crosby in Holiday Inn (1942) and then Blue Skies in 1946, the former features a brilliant solo dance by Fred to Let's Say It With Firecrackers. It's in Blue Skies that

Fred dances Puttin' On The Ritz, one of the songs that people will forever associate with him. Then in 1946 he announced he was to retire – but it did not last long. By 1949 Fred and Ginger were reunited in the film, The Barkleys Of Broadway, the only one of their films together to be shot in Technicolor.

It features a fantastic reprise of the Gershwins' They Can't Take That Away From Me, that had first been used in Shall We Dance in 1937.

Fred Astaire created his routines with other choreographers, but mostly with Hermes Pan. They, along with Ginger Rogers, revolutionised the Hollywood musical; they defined elegance for not just the generation of moviegoers from the 1930 but ever since. On every series of Strictly or Dancing With The Stars there are moments when the dancers

"ON EVERY SERIES OF STRICTLY OR DANCING WITH THE STARS THERE ARE MOMENTS WHEN THE DANCERS REPRISE ELEMENTS OF WHAT FRED AND GINGER DID, BUT NO-ONE WILL EVER DO IT BETTER"

Opposite *Fred Astaire and Ginger Rogers in Shall We Dance*

Bottom left *Bing Crosby*

Bottom right *Songwriting brothers George and Ira Gershwin*

reprise elements of what Fred and Ginger did, but no-one will ever do it better.

Throughout his movie career with Ginger, and later on with others, some of America's greatest composers wrote songs especially for Astaire to sing in his movies. The Gershwins, Irving Berlin and Jerome Kern, writers of The Great American Songbook, loved having Astaire do their songs in films as it guaranteed big sales.

But there was the added bonus of Astaire's singing. He's not the greatest singer in the world, does not have a fabulous range, but what he has is timing, maybe from his dancing. He delivers these songs with the same understated elegance as he and Ginger's dancing. After Astaire retired, Norman Granz, who later started Verve Records, recorded Fred and the Oscar Peterson reprising many of his finest songs from the films. A four-volume album was released as The Astaire Story and in 1999 it won the Grammy Hall of Fame Award.

"Ginger had never danced with a partner before Flying Down To Rio. She faked it an awful lot. She couldn't tap and she couldn't do this and that ... but Ginger had style and talent and improved as she went along. She got so that after a while everyone else who danced with me looked wrong." – Fred Astaire

And then along came Gene...

Of course, Astaire was not the only one making great dance movies after the 1930s. MGM got into the business after the decline of RKO's Thirties heyday under the leadership of Arthur Freed, who masterminded a move away from the old-fashioned style that people at the time thought Astaire's movies to be. In particular the use of Technicolor made a big difference, especially when they remade films from earlier times, like Show Boat featuring Marge and Gower Champion's dancing. There was a spate of musicals that came out of the MGM production unit including Easter Parade (1948), On The Town (1949), An American In Paris (1951), Singin' In The Rain (1952) and The Band Wagon (1953). Easter Parade starred Fred Astaire, while On The Town was an adaptation of a 1944 Broadway stage musical that was an adaptation of the Jerome Robbins choreographed ballet, Fancy Free; all of which feature music by Leonard Bernstein, who was 25 years old when he wrote the music for Fancy Free.

Ann Miller stars in On The Town and does a sensational dance number accompanied by Frank Sinatra, Jules Munshin and Gene Kelly – all three of them are playing drums. Gene Kelly gets fewer opportunities than in many of his films to show off his dancing skills but in the scene with Vera-Ellen, considered by many of her peers to be one of the best dancers from the era, called One Day In New York, he shines. Stylistically, it's a foretaste of what was to come in the later Kelly movies.

Born in Pittsburgh in 1912, Gene Kelly got his first Broadway break in Cole Porter's Leave It To Me! in 1938. A year later he got an even bigger break when he choreographed and danced in the Pulitzer Prize-winning The Time Of Your Life, which opened shortly after the outbreak of World War Two and a year later he truly became a star following his appearance on Broadway in Pal Joey.

Top right *Gene Kelly*

Right *A newspaper advert for On The Town*

Opposite *Gene Kelly in On The Town with Frank Sinatra, centre, and Jules Munshin*

M-G-M's MIRACLE MUSICAL HIT!

"ON THE TOWN"

(Technicolor)

It is challenging the phenomenal grosses of "Easter Parade" and topping M-G-M's Biggest!

*London's Empire Cinema in Leicester Square
at the UK premiere of Easter Parade*

➤ *"I don't believe in conformity to any school of dancing. I create what the drama and the music demand. While I am a hundred per cent for ballet technique, I use only what I can adapt to my own use. I never let technique get in the way of mood or continuity." – Gene Kelly, 1940*

Kelly's first movie appearance was with Judy Garland in For Me And My Girl in 1942 but his breakthrough as an on-screen dancer came two years later when he danced in the movie Cover Girl starring Rita Hayworth. In this film he dances with his own reflection in a shop window, it defines what made Kelly so brilliant. Aside from his technique, and his talent, he had such a brilliant imagination for choreography. His next film was Anchors Aweigh in 1945 in which MGM allowed him to devise his own dance routines that included the brilliant scene in which he dances with the animated and diminutive Jerry Mouse.

A year earlier he had starred with Fred Astaire in Ziegfeld Follies, although the film remained unreleased until 1946.

➤

Left *Gene Kelly with Rita Hayworth (right) in the 1944 American musical film Cover Girl*

Rita Hayworth during a photo shoot in London in April 1956

"GENE KELLY DID A STRING OF MOVIE APPEARANCES IN WHAT ARE AMONG THE BEST DANCE FILMS OF ALL TIME"

➤

The two geniuses dance to The Babbitt And The Bromide and it is a wonder to behold. If you've never seen it then you must. Again, it's YouTube to the rescue.

After wartime service Kelly was back in Hollywood to appear again with Judy Garland in the film version of S.N. Behrman's play The Pirate, with songs by Cole Porter.

Thirty-five-year-old Kelly's agility and fitness are incredible, especially in one of his best-remembered scenes, one with the Nicholas Brothers, two of the most brilliant dancers in the acrobatic school of dancing. If you watch any of the Nicholas Brothers routines you can see where break dancing and Michael Jackson took some of their inspiration.

Their dancing in Stormy Weather (1943), which also starred Lena Horne, is wonderful when they dance to the great Cab Calloway's music.

It was, according to Fred Astaire, "the greatest dance routine ever filmed", and it's certainly right up their with the very best. Every time I watch the bit where they jump off the piano and do the splits and get up without missing a beat my heart misses a beat.

Following the Pirate, Gene Kelly did a string of

movie appearances in what are among the best dance films of all time. In Words And Music, the 1948 film biography of composers Richard Rodgers and Lorenz Hart, there is a ballet danced by Gene Kelly and Vera-Ellen that is marvellous.

Summer Stock, Judy Garland's last musical film for MGM in 1950, has Kelly performing a routine to You, You Wonderful You in a darkened barn with a newspaper and a squeaky floorboard. Apparently, Kelly was amazing, spending time with Garland who was unwell, caused by her drug-taking, to get her scenes finished. Garland herself performed a brilliant routine to Get Happy in which she sings and dances and looks amazing, having lost 20lbs to get in shape to film.

Next up for Kelly came the two musicals, which have done more to crystallise his reputation than any of the others, An American In Paris in 1951 and the enduring Singin' In The Rain the following year. Kelly not only danced in these films but co-directed them and was the choreographer. Although we all know Singin' In The Rain it is An American In Paris that is a dancer's delight. So good was Kelly and his choreography so outstanding that the Academy of Motion Picture Sciences created a special Oscar that year in recognition of his achievement. It is based on George Gershwin's orchestral suite composed in 1928 and besides Kelly it also stars the beautiful Leslie Caron.

Top Leslie Caron in 1953, aged 21, rehearsing for a BBC TV show Toppers About Town held at the Trocadero in London. It was a reprise of her dance in An American In Paris

Above Judy Garland, arriving in Plymouth in April 1951 following her disembarkation from the transatlantic liner

Singin' in the Rain, besides featuring Kelly's famous solo routine to the title song, also includes the Moses Supposes routine with Donald O'Connor and as its fabulous finale, Broadway Melody, with Cyd Charisse. There were many more films after this that Kelly appeared in as well as directed but nothing ever reached the dizzy heights of his work in the six years after World War Two

Above The Cannes Film Festival, France, at a screening of That's Entertainment, Part 2 in May 1976. Cyd Charisse and Gene Kelly (left) with Fred Astaire and his daughter, Ava

"THAT'S ENTERTAINMENT EVOKES THE GLORY DAYS OF THE HOLLYWOOD MUSICAL – NOTHING BETTER IN MY BOOK"

Moira Shearer, aged 21 at the time, in a publicity shot issued at the time of The Red Shoes premiere

In 1976 I saw That's Entertainment, Part II which starred Kelly and his old friend Fred Astaire who Kelly managed to cajole into performing at 77 years old, despite Astaire having a contract ruling out any dancing. Astaire had, of course, long since retired and their performance of the title song, That's Entertainment, evokes the glory days of the Hollywood musical – nothing better in my book.

Gene Kelly was not the only star in this post-war era and among the best dance films ever made was in 1948, it was called The Red Shoes and it was made in Britain! It starred Moira Shearer, Anton Walbrook and Marius Goring and is a story within a story, being about a young ballerina who joins an established ballet company and then becomes the lead dancer in a new ballet called The Red Shoes; it was based upon a Hans Christian Andersen fairy story of the same name. Obviously it is not my kind of dancing, but it is another of those magical movies

➤

that captured the public's imagination. Oklahoma was an adaptation of Rodgers and Hammerstein's stage musical that had originally opened in 1943 and besides being made into a film in 1955 it has been revived on the stage on several occasions since. Following very much in the same vein were Guys And Dolls in 1955, Carousel and The King And I in 1956, and South Pacific and Gigi in 1958. All featured dancing but it was not central to the plot or the film. ➤

IT'S HERE!

The best-loved Musical Romance

of our time... now

a breath-taking motion picture

big as all outdoors!

RODGERS and HAMMERSTEIN'S

OKLAHOMA!

Starring
GORDON MacRAE
GLORIA GRAHAME
GENE NELSON • CHARLOTTE GREENWOOD
EDDIE ALBERT • JAMES WHITMORE
ROD STEIGER • SHIRLEY JONES

Directed by
FRED ZINNEMANN

Produced by
ARTHUR HORNBLOW JR.

Dances staged by
AGNES DeMILLE

Screen Play by
SONYA LEVIEN and WILLIAM LUDWIG

Music by
RICHARD RODGERS

Book and Lyrics by
OSCAR HAMMERSTEIN, II

A MAGNA PRODUCTION

Filmed in
CINEMASCOPE®

TECHNICOLOR®

The scene back stage, above left, during final dress rehearsals for the adaptation of Guys And Dolls at the Bristol Hippodrome in June 1953 and, left, the show's name in lights

One musical that was very different from all the rest was It's Always Fair Weather, which was released in 1955. It was different because it was a strangely downbeat affair in its subject matter but it did have some wonderful dancing – but then it would because Gene Kelly was in it and he co-directed it with Stanley Doran. It has music by André Previn and stars Gene Kelly, Dan Dailey, Cyd Charisse, Dolores Gray and Michael Kidd in his first film role. There is one wonderful scene where Kelly, Kidd and Dailey memorably dance with dustbin lids to a number called The Binge. It also has a fantastic scene on which Gene Kelly tap-dances on roller skates to I Like Myself; this is probably the last great dance solo of his career. It's a fitting place to finish this era of great dancing on film.

"ONE MUSICAL THAT WAS VERY DIFFERENT FROM ALL THE REST WAS IT'S ALWAYS FAIR WEATHER"

Above left Gene Kelly in his London hotel in October 1974

Above Cyd Charisse, who starred in It's Always Fair Weather

Let me tell you my West Side Story...

1962 was a momentous year for two reasons, Lorraine's Coffee Bar opened in Welling, which was near where I lived, in Kent, and on top of that I went to see West Side Story at the cinema.

I was going out with her girl who I had met at the Embassy Ballroom. We only went out together a few times but she was a really good dancer. I asked her if she'd like to go to the pictures, which was a big deal for me because I was only earning £2 10 shillings as an apprentice.

"Only if we can go and see West Side Story," she said.

From the opening sequence, which features the Sharks and the Jets, I was hooked and still am. Nothing can compare with the dancing in this film, for me it's one of the greatest films of all time and I've watched it umpteen times. I loved the songs as well – Somewhere, Something's Coming, Tonight, Maria and America take me back to that first time I watched the film at the Grenada in Welling.

Above *George Chakiris holds his Oscar for Best Supporting Actor in West Side Story in 1962, with the actress Shirley Jones*

Above right *Rita Moreno, pictured in 1964*

It's another movie with a score by Leonard Bernstein, a genius of modern American music – from classical to popular songs like those included in West Side Story. The words are by another brilliant composer, Stephen Sondheim. West Side Story started life as a Broadway show in 1957, came to London the following year and was filmed in 1961. It starred Natalie Wood, Richard Beymer, Rita Moreno, George Chakiris and Russ Tamblyn.

The plot is based around a troubled Manhattan neighbourhood, where a white American gang, the Jets, led by Riff (Russ Tamblyn), and a Puerto Rican gang, the Sharks led by Bernardo (George Chakiris). After a brawl that is broken up by the police, the Jets decide to challenge the Sharks to a fight for neighbourhood control at an upcoming dance.

It's full of great dance scenes, right from the very start of the movie, with the streets of New York as the backdrop. Living in Kent, New York seemed like it could be on another planet, and the Sharks and the Jets seemed very cool. It's hard to pick one number but Rita Moreno and Chakiris and the other dancers doing 'America' is as good as it gets.

"THE DANCE WITH DICK VAN DYKE AND THE PENGUINS HARKED BACK TO GENE KELLY'S GROUND-BREAKING SCENE IN ANCHORS AWEIGH, BUT IT'S STILL GREAT FUN"

The 1960s was a bit of a letdown after West Side Story, as far as dance movies was concerned. There were a few that captured the imagination, but to be honest they were mostly musicals that had a dance number or two in them, it was a bit of a throwback to the middle 1950s after the glory days of Gene Kelly.

One that everyone loves, of course, is Walt Disney's Mary Poppins that starred Dick Van Dyke and Julie Andrews. It's American take on East End life seemed a bit daft at times, but there was no doubting the effort that everyone put in to create wonderful set piece routines and some great tunes. The dance with Dick Van Dyke and the penguins harked back to Gene Kelly's ground-breaking scene in Anchors Aweigh, but it's still great fun.

Much befitting the mood of the era was a 1960s film starring Marilyn Monroe that was called Let's

20th CENTURY-FOX Presents

MARILYN MONROE
YVES MONTAND · FRANKIE VAUGHAN

JERRY WALD'S production of

LET'S MAKE LOVE "U"

COLOUR by DE LUXE

Co-starring **TONY RANDALL** with **WILFRID HYDE WHITE** Directed by **GEORGE CUKOR** Written for the screen by **NORMAN KRASNA** A **CINEMASCOPE** PICTURE

Let's Make Love, released in 1960, would be Marilyn Monroe's last film musical

Make Love. It would be Monroe's last film musical and co-starring with her is Yves Montand. It's a pretty improbable plot that also features cameos from Frankie Vaughan ("the singing idol of England" it says on the movie trailer), Gene Kelly and Bing Crosby. The scene which Marilyn does wearing just a jumper and a body stocking was pretty exciting at the time.

Years later I found out that Monroe and Montand had an affair while making the film, a very public one in fact, and she continued taking prescription drugs given to her all-too-readily by doctors while she was filming. But nothing takes away from Marilyn's performance when the camera was on her. It was one of the great tragedies that we lost her too soon.

"ONE OF THE HIGHLIGHTS OF THE FILM IS BILLY DOING 'TWIST KID', SUPPOSEDLY SET IN A SOHO NIGHTCLUB WITH DANCERS NATURALLY DOING THE TWIST"

➤

You will have noticed I skipped over all those 1950s rock and roll films in this chapter of the book.

Well, I am going to take a good long look at just how the music and the films of Bill Haley and many others changed the way we danced, and lived, in a later chapter.

However, I could not overlook another classic movie from 1962 – and a British one at that! Billy Fury was the biggest thing to have come out of Liverpool, up to that point at least, and he starred in a wonderful period

film in 1962 directed by Michael Winner. Called Play It Cool it also featured Helen Shapiro, Bobby Vee, Danny Williams and Shane Fenton, who later reinvented himself as Alvin Stardust!

One of the highlights of the film is Billy doing 'Twist Kid', supposedly set in a Soho nightclub with dancers naturally doing the Twist, or at least what they thought was the Twist. Lionel Blair and his dancers also appear and, while it lacks the Hollywood pizazz, it does have a certain charm.

(We're Gonna) Rock Around The Clock

Bill Haley looked less like what we all think of as a rock 'n' roller yet if you asked anyone to name just one rock and roll record they are more likely to say (We're Gonna) Rock Around The Clock than anything else.

Then again, it has sold more than 25 million copies, which is more than any other rock 'n' roll record. It's an anthem that has graced films – The Blackboard Jungle – countless wedding discos, TV shows – Happy Days – and kicked started countess radio shows in celebration of the 1950s and rock 'n' roll. It has all led to Bill being dubbed "the father of rock 'n' roll" and to us, today, he looks like it – but then again he was 29 years old when he had his first hit record.

(We're Gonna) Rock Around The Clock was written by Max C. Freedman and James Myers, the latter under the pseudonym Jimmy DeKnight; the song was actually first recorded by Sammy Dee and his Knights – no, I'd not heard of them either. Joe Turner also recorded a song called Around The Clock in 1946, although it has nothing musically to do with Haley's record. Bill's record topped the Billboard charts for eight weeks and also made No.1 in Britain.

Basically, it was this record that gave kids the idea that they might possibly rule the world, and they've never looked back!

"The rowdy element was represented by Rock Around The Clock theme song of the controversial film The Blackboard Jungle. The rock 'n' roll school in general concentrated on a minimum of melodic line and a maximum of rhythmic noise, deliberately competing with the artistic ideals of the jungle itself" – Encyclopaedia Britannica appraising Rock 'n' Roll in 1955.

Above Bill Haley in February 1957 at the Gaumont State cinema in Kilburn on his first tour of Britain

Right On a train to London's Waterloo station from Southampton, where he arrived by boat

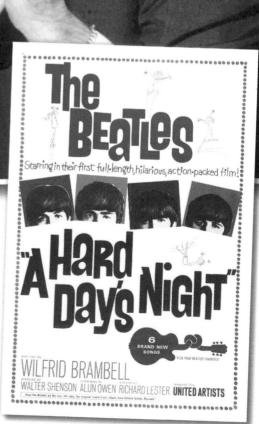

Just as Play It Cool was appearing in cinemas, The Beatles were auditioning for Parlophone Records; as we all know George Martin signed them and the world of music would never ever quite be the same again. The Beatles were just like Elvis and Cliff, as soon as they became stars, the first thing that happened was to get them into a film studio to capitalise on their success. In truth none of The Beatles' movies were really dance orientated but both A Hard Day's Night and Help! fuelled the whole Beatlemania craze that was sweeping the nation.

Opposite and below Paul McCartney with his Aunt Joan, and John Lennon with George Harrison's mum, at London's Dorchester Hotel after the premiere of A Hard Day's Night in 1964

Left Ringo Starr with Elizabeth Taylor at the Dorchester Hotel after a private screening of Around The World In 80 Days in March 1968

It's surprising, in a way, that there were not more dance films in the 1960s but probably the reaction to what had happened in the 1950s put a damper on things. Added to which, as soon as 1967 and the whole 'summer of love' thing came along and musicians, even pop ones, started taking themselves a bit too seriously.

So it wasn't until the 1970s that dance was back on our screens in a big way. It is a bit like the old cliché; sometimes things just have to skip a generation.

PAUL FRASER
CAMERAS

fortes
PRONTO BAR

12 SMASH SONG HITS!

*Premiere of A Hard Day's Night in July 1964.
While The Beatles may not have featured dancing
in their films, like everyone of their generation they
knew how to whirl a lady around the dance floor*

PEDESTRIANS
ASS AT LIGHTS
OR BY SUBWAY

Night Fever In Dartford!

When dance did come back on our cinema screens it did so with a bang, courtesy of the Bee Gees' amazing music and the on-screen presence of john Travolta. I'm talking about Saturday Night Fever of course. It is one of those films that undoubtedly did way better than anyone expected and its origins lay in a magazine article written by a British writer.

Nik Cohn wrote Tribal Rites Of The New Saturday Night in 1976 and later he admitted he had largely fabricated the story and based it on a Mod he knew in London – no not me!

The film itself came out at the end of 1977 and is all about Tony Manero (John Travolta), who spends his weekends at a Brooklyn disco. The Bee Gees' Stayin' Alive, which features over the opening credits of Travolta walking down a Brooklyn street, set the tone and the feel for the whole movie. Later in the movie when Travolta leads the dancers in the club to a routine to Night Fever it sparked the imagination of people all over the world. Disco was cool!

And Saturday Night Fever and Disco changed my life. In early 1978 I was a ballroom and Latin American dance teacher, that's what I loved and that's what I liked teaching. But everyone wanted to learn to dance like John Travolta and Karen Lynn Gorney and there was nowhere in Kent to learn the moves.

There was a young lad; Ken was his name, who was about nineteen who used to come to the dance school to help out. He went to see Saturday Night Fever over and over again and started to nag me about going to see it. He said we could teach people to dance like that. I went to see the film, I didn't like it much to be honest. It wasn't a case of 'cor what a film' but I took his point and we decided to try to capitalise on it.

We worked out some little things that we could teach and then put an advert in the paper. "You've seen the film; you've heard the music, now learn the dances. 'Saturday Night Fever' class, commencing next week."

Where do you go when the record is over...

SATURDAY NIGHT FEVER

Copyright © 1977 by Paramount Pictures Corporation. All Rights Reserved.

"SATURDAY NIGHT FEVER AND DISCO CHANGED MY LIFE. EVERYONE WANTED TO LEARN TO DANCE LIKE JOHN TRAVOLTA AND KAREN LYNN GORNEY"

Opposite *Demonstrating the dance moves made famous in Saturday Night Fever*

Well come the day and the hall was full, there were people down the flight of stairs that led up to my dance studio and half way up Dartford High Street. I ended up having to cancel loads of other classes just to fit in extra Saturday Night Fever fanatics – it was packed night after night. The fact was the school had not been bringing in huge amounts and while I wasn't quite down on my uppers but it revived my flagging finances.

When the movie Grease came along followed by Fame the floodgates opened; the seam of gold turned into a whole gold mine.

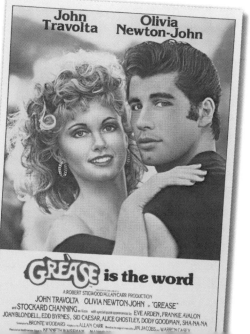

John Travolta   Olivia Newton-John

GREASE is the word

A ROBERT STIGWOOD/ALLAN CARR PRODUCTION

JOHN TRAVOLTA · OLIVIA NEWTON-JOHN in "GREASE"
and STOCKARD CHANNING as Rizzo with special guest appearances by EVE ARDEN, FRANKIE AVALON
JOAN BLONDELL, EDD BYRNES, SID CAESAR, ALICE GHOSTLEY, DODY GOODMAN, SHA-NA-NA
Screenplay by BRONTE WOODARD · Produced by ALLAN CARR · Based on the original musical by JIM JACOBS and WARREN CASEY

You're the one that I want...

Fresh from his success in Saturday Night Fever, John Travolta was snapped up to appear opposite Olivia Newton-John in Grease, which came out in the summer of 1978. Wallowing in the nostalgia of America of the 1950s and rock and roll music, with a 70s twist, it featured some great set piece numbers like Grease Lightning with the mechanics and Travolta strutting their stuff.

The most iconic scene from the film is Sandy (Newton-John) and Danny (Travolta) and the rest of the cast doing You're The One That I Want at the fairground. In many ways Grease owes much more to the Hollywood dance films of the 1940s and 1950s with its stylised set pieces…but what ever way you look at it, it is great fun.

The success of these two John Travolta films got every Hollywood studio looking for dance movie ideas and in 1980 along came Fame, although it is much more than just a dance film. Filmed from late summer onwards in 1979, it is based around a group of students and their studies at the New York High School of Performing Arts.

Something happens when she hears the music...
It's her freedom. It's her fire. It's her life.

Flashdance

What a feeling.

Take your passion and make it happen!

PARAMOUNT PICTURES PRESENTS A POLYGRAM PICTURES PRODUCTION · AN ADRIAN LYNE FILM · FLASHDANCE · JENNIFER BEALS · MICHAEL NOURI
MUSIC SUPERVISED BY PHIL RAMONE · EXECUTIVE PRODUCERS JON PETERS AND PETER GUBER · SCREENPLAY BY TOM HEDLEY AND JOE ESZTERHAS
STORY BY TOM HEDLEY · PRODUCED BY DON SIMPSON AND JERRY BRUCKHEIMER · DIRECTED BY ADRIAN LYNE · A PARAMOUNT PICTURE

The title song, sung by Irene Cara, won the Academy Award for Best Original Song, and the sequence with the kids dancing in the street certainly influenced more than a few videos over the coming decade as MTV became the driving force in American and later European music.

1983's Flashdance was much more of a dance film, as the title suggests. It was also a film that was critically panned but loved by cinemagoers. It's about Alex Owens (Jennifer Beals) an eighteen-year-old welder at a Pittsburgh steel mill who dreams of becoming a professional dancer. The climax is the audition dance to Flashdance – What A Feeling, sung by Irene Cara, that has become one of the most iconic dancing sequences from the 1980s.

What you may not know is that Jennifer Beales is not the dancer in the famous audition scene. Her main dance double is a French actress, Marine Jahan, while the breakdancing was done by the male dancer, aptly named Crazy Legs.

The famous slow-motion shot of Alex diving through the air is Sharon Shapiro, a professional gymnast. Just another example of you can't always believe what you see in films.

"IN MANY WAYS GREASE OWES MUCH MORE TO THE HOLLYWOOD DANCE FILMS OF THE 1940S AND 1950S WITH ITS STYLISED SET PIECES"

Top left *Olivia Newton-John and John Travolta*

Opposite *The cast of the stage version of Grease rehearsing at the New London theatre in 1973*

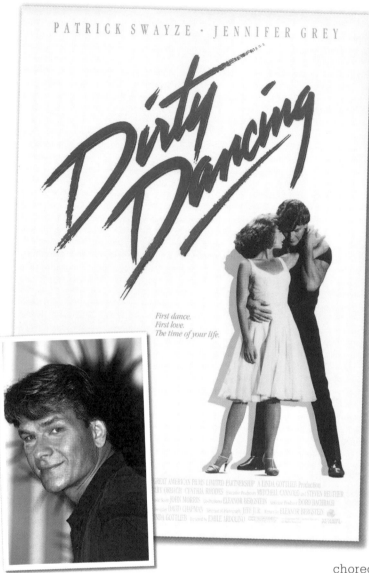

➤

From Flashdance to Footloose in 1984 and a dance movie of an altogether different kind. It tells the story of Kevin Bacon's character, a teenager from Chicago who moves to a small town where the local minister had banned rock music and dancing. Sound far fetched? Well apparently it actually happened. As you can imagine dancing wins and there are some big set piece dance numbers that culminate with the final sequence to the film's title song that is performed by Kenny Loggins.

Interestingly, the movie was remade in 2011 and it is fun to compare the two closing numbers, an updated version of Footloose. The original is still the best.

Three years after Footloose came one of the most popular dance movies of the modern era – Dirty Dancing. It has much more to do with more traditional dance movies than most of those from the previous decade. The closing scene where Patrick Swayze and Jennifer Grey dance to I've Had The Time Of My Life sung by Bill Medley and Jennifer Warnes is one that everyone in the world must have seen and enjoyed. It encapsulates everything that great dancing makes us feel. It's romantic and it features excellent choreography from the dancers; added to which it is so uplifting and not just in the way that Swayze lifts Jennifer Grey over his head.

In 2010, I met Jennifer because she appeared on Dancing With The Stars and after some fierce competition she and her partner Derek Hough won the series final.

"DIRTY DANCING ENCAPSULATES EVERYTHING THAT GREAT DANCING MAKES US FEEL. IT'S ROMANTIC AND IT FEATURES EXCELLENT CHOREOGRAPHY FROM THE DANCERS"

Above left Patrick Swayze and the poster promoting his famous film, Dirty Dancing

Left and top Scenes from the stage adaptation of Dirty Dancing

Above Actress Jennifer Grey attends the 25th anniversary screening of Dirty Dancing in 2012 in Los Angeles

A formation dance team in 1964. It's a look that has not changed over many decades

Hard lessons as life takes new turn…

It was shortly after we competed at the Royal Albert Hall in the Butlin's competition that Henry Kingston passed away. Joy, his widow, asked me shortly after that if I would turn professional and help her and Cherry run the dance school. It was a bit like asking one of the celebrities on Strictly Come Dancing to start teaching. We all know that necessity is the mother of invention, but this was ridiculous. But Joy was about to invent Britain's first ex-dock worker, come welder, dance teacher..

How I learned from class act

I began taking lessons from other teachers not only in dancing but in how to teach. The fact is that teaching is much more about experience than it is about knowing the steps. But you learn tricks and techniques from different teachers who all have their own way of doing things.

One of the best, if a little eccentric, teachers that I got to know was Len Scrivener. I got to know Len very well and a few years later I suggested he come with Cherry and me to Blackpool for the championships.

"I'll never step foot in that ballroom ever again," was all Len would say. He was a legend as a dancer

Blackpool's iconic tower and a pretty packed beach in 1952. It was always quieter when we went as it was during the off season

"THE FACT IS THAT TEACHING IS MUCH MORE ABOUT EXPERIENCE THAN IT IS ABOUT KNOWING THE STEPS"

and an extremely good teacher who the organisers would love to have had judging. Finally, I think it was in 1974, he relented and said he would grace Blackpool with his presence. That was only half the battle because his wife Nellie was adamant that she wasn't going and, whereas Len was self-educated and somewhat cultured, Nellie was a right gor blimey.

She eventually relented and we booked into Blackpool's The Clifton Hotel in Talbot Square and come the day of our departure I picked them up 8.30am to drive us north. At around eleven o clock we decided to stop for breakfast at the services on the M1, having parked up the four of us trooped into the place that had waitress service. I ordered a toasted tea cake and some tea, Cherry and Len said they'd have the same and Nellie said, " You know what? I'd like that early starter." This was a cooked breakfast special.

"Ah, I'm awfully sorry but you can only have the early starter until eleven."

These holidaymakers are seen dancing in Blackpool in 1958

Blackpool illuminations in September 1950

Blackpool was always a Mecca for dancing of every kind. This was in August 1958 at the Daily Mirror's Blackpool Week in August 1958

"Listen hear," says Len. "It's three minutes after eleven and my dear lady wife would like the early starter so surely you can rustle that up for her, please?"

"No I'm very sorry, it's only on until eleven o' clock," insisted the waitress. That was it, without another word Len stood up and started shouting.

"GET ME THE MANAGER. Bring him to me this instant."

It gave me an inkling into why he might have fallen out with the Blackpool people. Nevertheless, word had gone out that Len was going to the championships. It became the buzz of the dance world; the Messiah Scrivener is coming to Blackpool. Whatever his faults he was a genius at teaching. One day when we were learning the tango, for which there was no better teacher, he said to me, "Len the whole dance is lacking any atmosphere, you're just going through motions and there's no atmosphere."

"Well, what is atmosphere?" I asked Scrivener.

"Atmosphere is the outward expression of an inner emotion."

Isn't that brilliant? That's the kind of thing I learned from great teachers that helped me become a ballroom and Latin dance teacher.

Blackpool's famous illuminations have been an attraction for tourists since as far back as 1879. The first display, similar to the modern era, began in 1912. This photo dates from 1956

Cherry and me at the Royal Albert Hall in 1971 at what was called 'The Duel of the Giants'. It was us against a couple from Germany (that's them in the background). We won!

Mick on stage at Wembley's Empire Pool, as it was then called, in April 1965. Inset, the inside of Blackpool's Winter Gardens where there were regular dances. This photo shows the immediate aftermath of an appearance by the Rolling Stones in July 1964 when riots broke out

SONGS
THAT GOT BRITAIN
DANCING

Get Off My Cloud

By the time the Rolling Stones' eighth single came out we knew that Mick Jagger was a very special kind of performer, one who may have taken some of his moves from James Brown but when he danced he did so entirely in his own way.

Get Off My Cloud, when it came out in October 1965, filled dance floors in clubs and ballroom the length and breadth of Britain.

It topped the charts in both Britain and America, becoming the Rolling Stones' fifth No.1 in a row in the UK. The Stones recorded this, like many of their records at this time, in Hollywood and the sophistication of the production made it stand head and shoulders above other bands.

The fact that Mick is still prancing and dancing fifty years later is amazing. At their concerts over the past year he's shown no signs of slowing up. He proves that if you stay fit and healthy you can dance on. Power to you, Mick!

A formation of Germans

Early on in my dance teaching days a German couple came to our dance school and, after several visits, they asked Cherry and me if we would be prepared to go and teach in Germany, for a lot more money than we could make in Britain. They wanted us to train their formation dance team in Dusseldorf. I immediately said yes. The only drawback, as Cherry pointed out as soon as they had left, was the fact that we'd never done any formation team dancing, let alone training. I had never even watched it. If the formation came on, I went to the bar.

"Yes I know but for fifty quid an hour we can learn."

I taught the team for three days and changed some bits around, it was actually quite straightforward. I found different pattern changes, easy steps and

Formation dancing is all about precision, from the choreography to the way the team dances; it's also about the matching dresses and the stylish look of a team

quickly realised that I saw it all in my head as I talked about it. To explain more easily where the dancers needed to be in order to make patterns on the dance floor I used eight penny coins – the big ones, pre-decimalization. As I moved the coins around the table I'd say: "Right, you two are going to go up there and you two are going there." But even I was surprised a month later when we got a telegram saying they'd won the German championships, previously they had never come better than third.

For years and years Cherry and I went to Germany for three days every two weeks to train their formation team, take classes and give private lessons. They bought our house and made us a small fortune.

When I was working for the American insurance company they sent me on a course and one of the things a trainer said very definitely applied to this situation. "Success comes in cans, not in can'ts."

"FOR YEARS AND YEARS CHERRY AND I WENT TO GERMANY FOR THREE DAYS EVERY TWO WEEKS TO TRAIN THEIR FORMATION TEAM"

Twist And Shout

The Beatles, like so many other groups from the 'Beat Boom' era, made records that teenagers loved to dance to. The Beatles and other bands looked to America to find songs that they could cover. Now you're going to say, but Lennon and McCartney wrote Love Me Do, Please, Please Me, From Me To You and She Loves You, which is true. But on their first album, Please, Please Me, six of the fourteen songs are cover versions.

Shortly before 10am on Monday, February 11, 1963, The Beatles arrived at Abbey Road Studios in London to begin work on their first long-playing record. Ten hours later, it was all but finished, except for George Martin doing a few overdubs two days later.

They recorded ten of the fourteen tracks for Please, Please Me that day, and were in the middle of a tour with Helen Shapiro, playing two shows every night, travelling from show to show the length and breadth of Britain. Truth is that when they arrived at Abbey Road they were knackered, so much so that there were doubts in the mind of producer George Martin that they could last the two sessions they were booked to do, let alone the three that they ended up doing.

After working all day, and just before the 10pm curfew imposed by Abbey Road Studios, they did one more song, and in one take nailed Twist And Shout. The Phil Medley and Bert Berns – although it's credited to Bert Russell – song had been a hit for the Isley Brothers, having originally been recorded as Shake It Up Baby by the Top Notes.

The Beatles had to do it in one take because John's voice was so shot, he had a bad cold, that he could only do the one vocal. It was a defining number in The Beatles' early career and remains one of the great rock vocals of all time. And it is the record that I think of when it comes to dancing from that era of beat groups… "shake it up baby, now, twist and shout!"

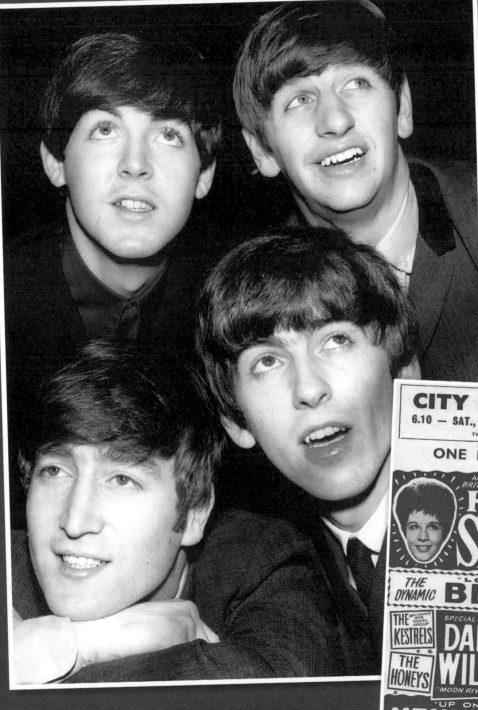

John, Paul, George and Ringo pictured on February 10, 1963, the day before they recorded Twist And Shout

Left The Beatles on stage in Plymouth on November 13, 1963

CITY HALL · SHEFFIELD
6.10 — SAT., 2nd MARCH, 1963 — 8.40
TWO PERFORMANCES ONLY

ONE NIGHT ONLY

ARTHUR HOWES PRESENTS
BRITAIN'S INTERNATIONAL TEENAGE STAR

HELEN SHAPIRO

THE DYNAMIC "LOVE ME DO" BEATLES

THE GRIFFIN'S ACE VOCAL GROUP
KESTRELS

SPECIAL GUEST STAR
DANNY WILLIAMS
"MOON RIVER" "JEANNIE"

THE RED PRICE BAND

THE HONEYS

YOUR COMPERE
DAVE ALLEN

"UP ON THE ROOF"
KENNY LYNCH

PRICES 8/6 7/- 6/6 5/6 5/- 4/- 3/6
Booking Agents : Wilson Peck Ltd., 78-84 Fargate, Sheffield

A rock and roll dancing competition at Nottingham Palais in 1956

CHAPTER 7

Rocking all over the dance floor

I was just a little young boy when rock 'n' roll first hit our shores but I quickly got to love the music, who wouldn't? The best rock 'n' roll is so infectious, so upbeat and the best songs cannot help but get you out of your seat and on to the dance floor. When Bill Haley arrived in Britain he was 32 years old, hardly a teenage idol, and he looked even older. But such was the magic of the music that he caused something of a scandal with everyone from church leaders to Encyclopedia Britannica declaring rock and roll dancing was especially sinful.

America's rock 'n' roll invasion of Britain

Rock and roll is as old as mankind and the first rock 'n' roll record was Jackie Brenston and his Delta Cats' Rocket 88, recorded at Sam Phillips' Sun Studios in Memphis, Tennessee.

One of these two things is untrue – it's not that rock and roll is as old as mankind. Rock 'n' roll was little more than a euphemism among the black population in early 20th century America, as blues singer Trixie Smith sang, "My man rocks me with one steady roll." I think you get the idea!

For most people, especially in Britain, Bill Haley is the man that started it all. He had his first British hit in December 1954, when he topped the British charts with (We're Gonna) Rock Around The Clock at the end of 1955 and went on to have a string of hits before he visited Britain in 1957.

The man who started out playing country music certainly has a lot to answer for. His legacy is assured and while he never perhaps looked the part he always sounded it.

"ROCK 'N' ROLL WAS LITTLE MORE THAN A EUPHEMISM AMONG THE BLACK POPULATION IN 20TH CENTURY AMERICA"

Bill Haley and his Comets at the Hammersmith Palais in February 1957

The Gaumont State cinema in Kilburn, February 7, 1957

After watching the film Rock Around The Clock at the cinema, some teenagers were arrested when they began to riot in September 1956

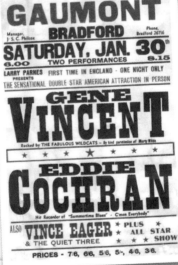

Homegrown rock and roll

O f course there was also Elvis, the great Buddy Holly, Gene Vincent and Eddie Cochran and a string of others that all made great rock and roll records which were firm favourites on jukeboxes everywhere.

In Britain we had some homegrown rock and roll talent that definitely borrowed from their American counterparts but did their best to sound original.

It was The 2 I's that was the most famous coffee bar in London, and it is often called the birthplace of British rock and roll. Cliff Richard and The Drifters got a booking at Soho's 2 I's coffee bar. It was at the 2 I's that Cliff first met a 21-year-old guitarist named Ian Samwell who soon after joined The Drifters; Samwell wrote one of, if not, the best British rock and roll dance record, Cliff's Move It.

Among those who had used the coffee bar as a springboard to success was Tommy Steele who in

Below *Jiving at the 2 I's Coffee Bar in the late 1950s*

Below right *Cliff Richard in 1958*

"IT WAS THE 2 I'S THAT WAS THE MOST FAMOUS COFFEE BAR IN LONDON, AND IT IS OFTEN CALLED THE BIRTHPLACE OF BRITISH ROCK AND ROLL"

two short years had already scored with a string of British hit records that were, according to Cliff Richard, not really rock and roll records but some kind of pale British imitation of the real thing.

Soho was Mecca for coffee bars; the first was The Moka in Frith Street that was opened by the actress Gina Lollabrigida in 1953. They all had names that somehow sounded exotic – The Arabica, The Bamboo, and The Mocamba were all in London. The cafes attracted CND activists, the jazz crowd, and rock 'n' rollers all eager for an espresso or a cappuccino, which most of us back then called a frothy coffee. In many of these Soho coffee bars and clubs there was dancing.

Right
Tommy Steele plays and this young lady jives!

SINGING... DANCING... ACTING...
IN A **FABULOUS DUAL-ROLE!**

Hear TOMMY's latest SMASH HIT TUNES!

TOMMY STEELE

The **DUKE WORE JEANS**

Co-starring
MICHAEL MEDWIN
with ALAN WHEATLEY
ERIC POHLMANN
CLIVE MORTON

AND **JUNE LAVERICK** as "The Princess"

Produced by PETER ROGERS
Directed by GERALD THOMAS   Based on a Story by LIONEL BART & MICHAEL PRATT
Screen Play by NORMAN HUDIS
ANGLO AMALGAMATED FILM DISTRIBUTORS, Ltd

GENERAL RELEASE NOW

The epitome of 1950s cool!

Left Phil Chicken shows his rock 'n' roll moves at a revival event in Tyneside in 1974

Below left Rockers enjoying a lively night out at the Crown and Anchor in Brixton in 1956

Below right Teenagers rock 'n' roll dancing at a Cardiff dance hall in 1957

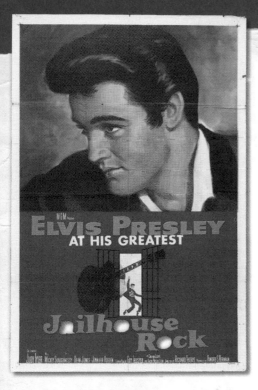

Jailhouse Rock

As soon as you hear those opening chords it's like someone shouting, "Come on! Let's get on the dance floor". Elvis Presley's Jailhouse Rock came out in America in late September 1957 to coincide with the release of his motion picture of the same name. In Britain it was released a few months later and it topped the UK singles chart at the end of January 1958, becoming the best-selling record of the whole year.

Jailhouse Rock, written by Jerry Leiber and Mike Stoller, features in the film during a fantastic scene where Elvis and the other jailbirds dance; it is all very reminiscent of earlier Hollywood musicals, except the music is so very different. Leiber and Stoller wrote a string of great rock and roll records including Yakety Yak, Spanish Harlem, Love Potion No.9, Stand By Me and Hound Dog.

In The Blues Brothers film it was the closing song in the movie as Dan Aykroyd and John Belushi perform it in prison and the place erupts into a huge dance.

It was March 2, 1960, and Elvis Presley made his one and only visit to Britain. He was on his way home from his home having completed his Army service in Germany when his aircraft touched down at Prestwick Airport in Scotland for a refueling stop. Hundreds of fans greeted the retiring Sergeant Elvis Presley and he apparently whispered to an Air Force lieutenant, "where am I?" The photo was taken the day before at a press conference in Germany. Pictured with Elvis is Donald Zec, the Daily Mirror's show business correspondent

After the Encyclopaedia Britannica condemned The Blackboard Jungle it was perhaps inevitable that films aimed at teenagers, and with rock and roll as their soundtrack, would catch on in a big way. These films, like most other musicals before them, all had dancing in them and their soundtracks spawned hit singles; they also encouraged many young people to dance.

It's all a long way from ballroom dancing but to me it doesn't matter how you get people dancing, it's getting them dancing that is important. Once they are through the door of a disco, club, dance hall, holiday camp, or a ballroom and get a love for dancing, who knows where it will lead.

Here's a selection of some of the best films from the rock and roll era and all of them feature dancing to some degree or another:

Rock Around The Clock (1956)
Don't Knock The Rock (1956),
inspired by Bill Haley's 1956 hit single
Rock, Rock, Rock (1956)
Shake Rattle And Roll (1956)
Mister Rock and Roll (1957)
The Girl Can't Help It (1957)
King Creole (1958)

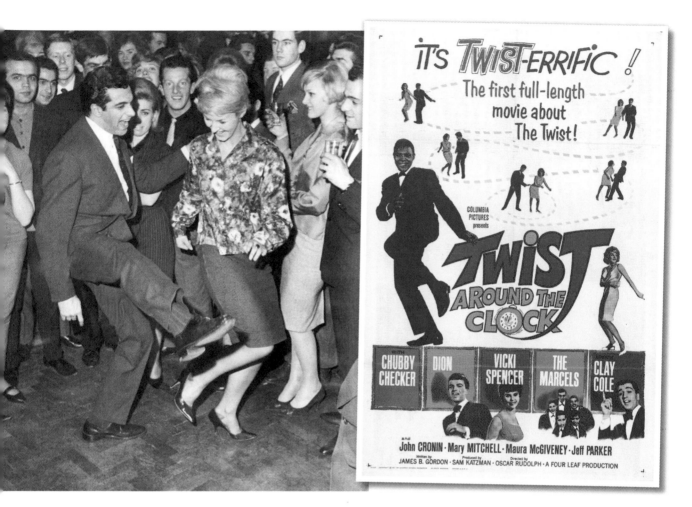

Dancing with a twist

With the arrival of rock 'n' roll, dance crazes proliferated like never before. An American singer named Bobby Freeman was the first to record Do You Wanna Dance. In Britain, Cliff covered it and it seemed like we all did! In 1960, Chubby Checker released The Twist and dancing mania really took hold.

In the wake of The Twist there was, or so it seemed, a new dance craze every month. Most of them seemed to be invented in America and many of of them made it across the Atlantic – Wilson Picket was right, it was a 'Land of a 1000 Dances'!

Here's my list, can you think of any more?

The Madison, The Bunny Hop, The Mashed Potato, The Stroll, The Shimmy, The Monster Mash, Hitch Hike, The Hully Gully, The Loco-Motion and The Monkey.

Above left Frankie Vaughan at a 'London Twist club' and he not only knows how to do it, he has written a Twist song, said the caption in January 1962

"WITH THE ARRIVAL OF ROCK 'N' ROLL, DANCE CRAZES PROLIFERATED LIKE NEVER BEFORE"

Dancing the twist on a boat crossing the English Channel to Calais, June 1962

You have to read the caption in the voice of those old newsreel announcers. "A new dance which is the rage in America has now come to London. It is called the 'twist'. These pictures show some of the steps and actions of the dance and were taken at The Satire Club in Duke of York Street, London, S.W.I. in October 1961"

Left
Lionel Blair at The Café de Paris demonstrating the 'New' Madison in September 1962

Below
Demonstrating the Madison

A rock and roll evening at Belle Vue in Manchester in the 1950s

Let's Twist Again

SONGS THAT GOT BRITAIN DANCING

Chubby Checker was born in 1941 as plain old Ernest Evans. With a name like that he could have come from the East End of London but he was born in South Carolina and grew up in a tough part of South Philadelphia. His version of The Twist, originally a hit in America in 1960 for its writer Hank Ballard, topped the US charts in September of the same year. So popular was the whole twist dance phenomena that Checker's record went back to top of the American charts in January 1962 – the only record to ever achieve such a feat.

In Britain, The Twist could only make the Top 40 in 1960. It took a while for the dance craze to catch hold in the UK. Chubby Checker went to No.2 in Britain with Let's Twist Again'in early 1962; strangely it only made No.8 in America but that was probably because the twist craze had waned somewhat, new dances had come along.

Chubby Checker showing how the twist is really done when he visited Britain in September 1962

The Dance Rage from USA

THE TWIST

SONG COPY with DANCE STEPS
2/- Post 3d.

ORCHESTRATIONS 4/6d. Post 4d.

Recorded by CHUBBY CHECKER
on COLUMBIA

★

Published by LOIS MUSIC LTD.
subsidiary of
PETER MAURICE MUSIC CO. LTD.
21 Denmark St., London, W.C.2. TEMple Bar 3856

A rock and roll event on Blackpool's pier drew huge crowds in the summer of 1960, with plenty of dancers willing to strut their stuff

*Inside the majestic
Blackpool Tower Ballroom*

CHAPTER 8

The places where we all had a ball...

Ballrooms have always been magical places for me and some, even now, just take your breath away. But try to imagine how amazing these places were in the first half of the century, in their hey day. Our homes have become much more comfortable since then, and so the contrast between people's home lives and a magnificent ballroom are not as great. Ballrooms were originally found in the mansions of the very rich, and so it was natural that when public ballrooms were first built they were often modelled on the private ballrooms. Mirrors, gilding, lights and opulence were the order of the day...

Blackpool was the pinnacle for me...

Throughout my career as a dancer and later on as a judge I have been lucky enough to set foot in some of the best ballrooms in the world. Some people think that before I started judging on Strictly Come Dancing and Dancing With The Stars in America that I just used to dance but I've judged all over the world.

I used to regularly judge in Japan and at the United States Ballroom Championships, which are in Miami every September. Then, in 1993, I was asked to judge the open section of the Blackpool Championships, which is the pinnacle of a judge's achievement. I'd previously judged the exhibition section. I judged Junior Blackpool, the Closed

Below *Newcastle's Oxford Galleries in 1960*

Right *According to the caption on the original photo, "The ladies' powder room at the Lacarno Ballroom in Coventry. Each mirror has a bracket light and a shelf for cosmetics." Taken in August 1960, this was the height of sophistication*

"JUDGING BLACKPOOL BRINGS YOU FAR MORE KUDOS THAN JUDGING THE WORLD CHAMPIONSHIPS"

Above *Me judging sometime in the late 1980s. I judged dance competitions all over the world*

National British Championships, but I had never actually judged the premier dancing competition in the world.

When they finally asked me I was so excited because judging Blackpool brings you far more kudos than judging the world championships, which I'd already done. In those days there was a panel of eleven judges that adjudicated at each event and these were drawn from a pool of twenty-five judges. In the dance world it's a bit like becoming a Knight of the Garter, it's certainly a very select group. From a career point of view this was it, I was in with the most respected judges in the dance world – once you've judged Blackpool you've cracked it. I was even asked back several more times during the nineties, so I must have been doing something right. Although I'm making a joke of it I was very proud of this and still am – it's a great honour.

The Old Assembly Rooms
in Newcastle in 1952

Above The former Orchid Ballroom in Coventry had been made into a bingo hall in the 1960s, a fate that befell many a ballroom. Here it was being converted back into a club and venue for dancing and concerts in 1990

Left The dance floor at the Locarno in Coventry is packed as balloons fall down to mark the start of the new year in 1966

Top The ceiling of the Rivoli Ballroom in South London where I danced on many occasions

Above The Belle Vue Ballroom in Manchester in November 1958

Left The Locarno Ballroom in Birmingham in August 1960

Night Fever

Both the album Saturday Night Fever and the single Night Fever rank among the biggest-selling records of all time.

When Robert Stigwood, the Bee Gees manager and producer of the film, first put the idea of providing the music for a new film about the disco phenomenon in New York he was calling the movie Saturday Night. According to Robin Gibb, "Robert Stigwood wanted to call the film Saturday Night, and we had already written the song Night Fever. "We told him we didn't like the title Saturday Night and he said he didn't want to call the movie just Night Fever. So he thought it over for a while, called us back, and said, 'OK, let's compromise. Let's call it Saturday Night Fever. We said, 'All right, that's great. So we'll keep it at that'."

To get some idea of how big a song Night Fever became it was No.1 on the Billboard Hot 100 single for over two months in 1978; that is an almost unheard-of feat.

To give you a an idea of how successful Barry, Robin and Maurice were at this time, they replaced their brother Andy Gibb's Love Is Thicker Than Water at No.1 and Night Fever was, in turn, replaced by Yvonne Elliman's If I Can't Have You – which was also from the Saturday Night Fever soundtrack. All three songs were written and produced by the Gibb brothers. It also topped the charts in the UK and in many other countries around the world.

Night Fever is just such an infectious song; the rhythm is just perfect for the style of dancing that took over the world in 1978. It's one of the songs that as soon as it is played men of a certain age strike the pose, one arm in the air and in their own minds look not unlike a 23-year-old John Travolta.

Robin, Barry and Maurice Gibb shortly after the Saturday Night Fever era

Meccas for Moderns

If the inside of ballrooms can be breathtakingly beautiful the exteriors are sometime a little plain, especially during the daytime. At night when the lights go on they do sparkle a little bit more, but maybe that's all part of the allure of their interiors. Often ballrooms were placed in city centres and the buildings around them have changed. Others were built when cities were rebuilt.

Some like Rivoli in Tooting have been unchanged for years. It is London's only remaining original 1950s ballroom and I danced there hundreds of times over the years. Its beautiful interior has featured in films, video shoots and in more recent times rock bands have also used it for concerts. It was originally a cinema and was converted to a dance hall in the late 1950s, but looks much older.

Right *London's Hammersmith Palais, pictured in 1970, has now been demolished but is just one of hundreds of ballrooms I have visited*

Below *The Rivoli Ballroom*

Below right *Tiffany's in Coventry, seen here in January 1983, is an example of the new-style ballrooms that appeared from the 1970s onwards*

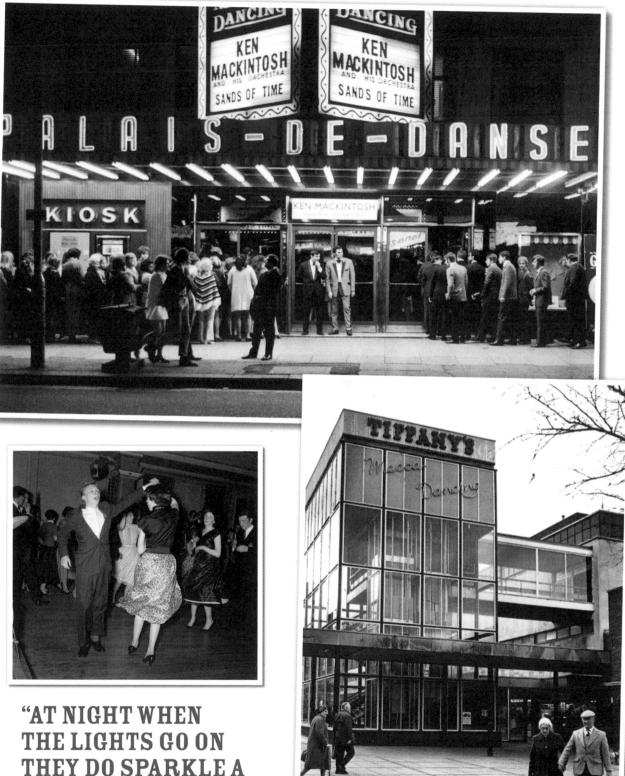

"AT NIGHT WHEN THE LIGHTS GO ON THEY DO SPARKLE A LITTLE BIT MORE"

Ballrooms come in all shapes and sizes. This is the Pier Ballroom, on Redcar seafront, in 1973

This is the scene from a short film called Mods And Rockers that was made at Twickenham Studios in July 1964. The music for the film was by The Cheynes, Mick Fleetwood's band before Fleetwood Mac

CHAPTER 9

Turning on style as music scenes strike a chord

The dance crazes that swept through Britain in the early 1960s went almost as quickly as they came. There was little time for fashion to keep pace with them. When the Mod era arrived the fashion was an integral part of 'the scene' and dressing stylishly was everything, much like the singers and artists from Tamla Motown who always looked stylish. By the time the whole glam and glitter period arrived fashion was completely bound up with the music and became integral. It was the same when Saturday Night Fever gave rise to disco...

Entering the Mod-ern era...

I was a Mod but I only recently found out the term has its roots in 1950s Modern Jazz when people listening to the kind of music released by Blue Note Records were dubbed Modernists – or Mods.

The Mod movement had its origins in London and soon these men and women who revered smart clothes, particularly Italian suits for men, Italian made scooters – Lambrettas and Vespas – and dancing at all-nighters in clubs were, by the mid-1960s, being seen all over Britain.

While a love of fashion was key to all things Mod, music formed a vital part of the culture. It was black music that Mods danced to in clubs like the Marquee, La Discothèque, The Flamingo and their

The Supremes, from left, Florence Ballard, Mary Wilson and Diana Ross, each with a Polaroid Camera, arrive in London to appear in Ready, Steady, Go! and Thank Your Lucky Stars in October 1965

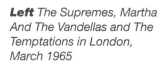

Left The Supremes, Martha And The Vandellas and The Temptations in London, March 1965

Below Young Mods, hands clasped behind their backs, do a dance someone on the original caption dubbed, 'the Prince Philip dance'. The band is the Dave Clark Five and it was taken in Basildon, Essex, in August 1963

"WHILE A LOVE OF FASHION WAS KEY TO ALL THINGS MOD, MUSIC FORMED A VITAL PART OF THE CULTURE"

spiritual home, the hottest of the hot, The Scene Club in London's Ham Yard. Today, most people see The Who as synonymous with Mod culture. The Who's music was embraced by regional Mods, way more than the London Mods – we thought of ourselves as a cut above our provincial comrades.

It was black music that included Motown, Stax Records and Jamaican Ska that every Mod loved and, of course, danced to. Motown's tours of the UK and their early assault on the British charts with The Supremes, Martha And The Vandellas and Marvin Gaye – the sharpest dresser among Motown's sharpest dressers. Suits you Sir, and it did!

Ready to go for a great time...

Staged by Ready, Steady, Go!, the Mod Ball at the Empire Pool Wembley, as it used to be called, took place in April 1964. It featured the Rolling Stones, Cilla Black, Freddie and the Dreamers, Sounds Incorporated, Kenny Lynch, Kathy Kirby, Manfred Mann Fourmost, Billy J.Kramer & the Dakotas, Merseybeats, and the Searchers with comperes Keith Fordyce & Cathy McGowan.

According the Daily Mirror, "It was the noisiest, screamingest crowd we have ever had at the Empire Pool. The Stones were mobbed as they left the stage. Commissionaires fought to protect them."

Below Dancing at the Mod Ball at Wembley's Empire Pool in April 1964

Right Another photo of the Mod Ball, see it wasn't all mini skirts in the Sixties!

Below right Sounds Incorporated on stage at the Mod Ball

"IT WAS THE
NOISIEST,
SCREAMINGEST
CROWD WE HAVE
EVER HAD AT
THE EMPIRE
POOL"

9.53 Ready, Steady, Go! Mod Ball

This is the night of the year when 8,000 mods (note for squares: mods are the smartest fashion-conscious teenagers) congregate in aid of children's charity in the **Empire Pool, Wembley,** to dance to the top pop names. It's a live show in every sense of the word. Stand by for excitement!

INTRODUCED BY
KEITH FORDYCE
WITH
Cathy McGowan
AND
Michael Aldred

CILLA BLACK
The **FOURMOST**
FREDDIE and the **DREAMERS**
KATHY KIRBY
BILLY J. KRAMER and the **DAKOTAS**
KENNY LYNCH
MANFRED MANN
The **MERSEYBEATS**
The **ROLLING STONES**
The **SEARCHERS**
SOUNDS INCORPORATED

PROGRAMME EDITOR FRANCIS HITCHING
EXECUTIVE PRODUCER
ELKAN ALLAN

Above The Rolling Stones on stage at the Mod Ball show

Left The artists at the Mod Ball at Wembley's Empire Pool in April 1964

*The Rolling Stones'
Brian Jones and
Bill Wyman sign
autographs at the
Mod Ball event
and, below, the
band on stage*

Dancing In The Street

Martha And The Vandellas' Dancing In The Street, which was co-written by Marvin Gaye, is the perfect Motown dance record – infectious, great words, great musicians and at two minutes 38 seconds it packs the perfect punch.

Dancing In The Street demonstrates exactly what it is that makes Motown's records so great, and it starts with their tried and trusted formula – an attention-grabbing first ten seconds. The intro with Martha singing, "Calling out around the world" is irresistible. And call out she certainly did when this record burst out from our transistor radios in in the autumn of 1964.

Every self-respecting Mod loved it!. But not everyone else did as it only made No.28 on the UK charts; it was reissued in 1969 and on that occasion made the top five.

Berry Gordy, who founded Motown, had a

Recorded by MARTHA and THE VANDELLAS on Gordy Records
DANCING IN THE STREET
By WILLIAM STEVENSON and MARVIN GAYE

simple strategy; it was to make his records appeal to everyone, black or white, which is how and why he came up with the slogan – the Sound of Young America.

The truth was Britain embraced Motown from the very start and it had a great deal to do with the fact that every record was perfect for dancing.

While 'the sound' of Motown appeared to be simple, it was pop music of an incredibly sophisticated kind.

Some have called it 'assembly-line pop', no doubt moved to do so through it's connection to Detroit – the motor city – Motown. Yet Gordy and his small team managed to make each record sound like it had been hand crafted. 'Hitsville', which is what he called the Motown HQ, very soon became a hit-factory.

Glitter and glam

Pop music has never been short of new ways of reinventing itself and so very often it is on the back of, or by latching onto, the latest dance craze. After the 'summer of love' in 1967 and the coming of rock music in the 1969, which took itself very seriously, there was a need for a return to fun.

Along came glitter and glam rock, the era of Marc Bolan and T. Rex along with David Bowie, who managed to make great records that were also fun, put people make on their feet and dancing was once again in.

Right *David Bowie and wife Angie with their three-week old baby Zowie in June 1971. I wish this photo had been in colour because the original caption says that he is wearing 44-inch Oxford Bags in pink seaside gabardine*

> "ALONG CAME GLITTER AND GLAM ROCK, THE ERA OF MARC BOLAN AND T. REX ALONG WITH DAVID BOWIE"

David Bowie as 'Ziggy Stardust' in May 1973

Marc Bolan of T. Rex in January 1974

Above *The Slack Alice nightclub in Manchester, which belonged to George Best. It's February 1976 and as you can see from the fashions this was at the tail end of glitter and on the cusp of disco...boiler suits were never a good look*

Right *Slade, seen here rehearsing for Top Of The Pops in 1973, was another band from the era of glam rock that had everyone dancing*

On stage in May 1973 there was Grease and it featured a very young Richard Gere as Danny Zuko (left in denim shirt) seen here in rehearsal with the rest of the cast

Above *There may not be much glitter, but you have to admit it was glamorous! In May 1972 Air Canada had introduced Boeing 747s on their route from Toronto to London. In an effort to attract more passengers, they installed a dance floor and taped music for passengers who would like to dance at 30,000 ft on their way across the Atlantic*

Disco fever

The Saturday Night Fever film started showing across the UK in March 1978 and it created an explosion in disco. As I've already said it was not my favorite kind of dancing but there was no doubting it captured the public's imagination. It wasn't just my little dance school in Dartford that rode the wave, it seemed like discos were opening everywhere, and people no longer went to a dance, they went to a disco.

It was in late April 1978 that the Bee Gees went to No.1 with Night Fever and they were followed over the course of the next year by a string of disco records including Boney M's Rivers Of Babylon

➤

Disco fever grips the contestants in the World Disco Championships at the Empire Leicester Square in December 1978

Boney M pictured in
November 1968

"IT SEEMED LIKE DISCOS WERE OPENING EVERYWHERE, AND PEOPLE NO LONGER WENT TO A DANCE, THEY WENT TO A DISCO"

Above The fashions were interesting and the dancing was clearly influenced by John Travolta, as can be seen here at the Winter Gardens, Cleethorpes, Lincolnshire, in April 1978

Right The original caption says, 'Birmingham's own John Travolta, Graham Methoo seen here after a daily visits to Birmingham's Corinthians Fitness Centre. Graham is pictured dancing to a disco version of Singing In The rain'. It was April 1978

➤

(five weeks at No.1), You're The One That I Want by John Travolta and Olivia Newton-John from Grease that spent nine weeks at the top, Rod Stewart's D'Ya Think I'm Sexy; The Village People YMCA and I Will Survive Gloria Gaynor. To say nothing of a string of other big-selling records which usually managed to get the word 'disco' in the title.

Right *The Village People. Is there anyone who has not done the YMCA dance, with the actions?*

Below *Chic produced some of the best dance records from the period. Seen here in the UK promoting Le Freak, from left, Tony Thompson, Bernard Edwards, Alfa Anderson, Luci Martin and Nile Rodgers in January 1979*

Filming a BBC variety show at the Wood Green Empire in January 1957

CHAPTER 10

Always moving with the times

The BBC produced a report in the 1940s in which it announced that while radio could be listened to in the background, the television "demands your attention" and there was a limit to the amount of time "an ordinary viewer can give to his viewing". There would therefore be no need, it decided, but to broadcast for limited periods in the afternoons and evenings. However, its report specifically talked about "variety, cabaret and ballet" all being regularly broadcast on the BBC, and dancing in one way or another has been on our TV screens ever since, with every kind of style being featured.

Victor Silvester's Dancing Club

Victor Silvester appeared on the radio throughout the war, hosting his programme BBC Dancing Club. These programmes were broadcast from the Paris Cinema in Lower Regent Street, London, before a studio audience.

When television began broadcasting after the war, BBC Dancing Club was one of the shows that transferred from radio to television in 1948.

In 1953, the show was broadcast from the Carlton Rooms, Maida Vale, London. It featured professional dancing couples, including, Andé Lyons and Walter Laird, and Frank and Peggy Spencer, with some of the top amateur dancers also appearing.

"BBC DANCING CLUB WAS ONE OF THE SHOWS THAT TRANSFERRED FROM RADIO TO TELEVISION IN 1948"

Behind the scenes on Victor Silvester's BBC Dancing Club

Everyone enjoying a cuppa, nowadays it would be a bottle of water in everyone's hand

Victor Silvester and some of the dancers being photographed in 1954

Come Dancing

Above The West Midlands formation team appearing
in Come Dancing with music was provided by Alan
Ross and his Orchestra in December 1962

Below Members of the Wales team who were
defeated by just one point by the Home Counties
South team in the semi-final of Come Dancing, held
at the City Hall, Cardiff in February 1968

Come Dancing was created by Eric Morley in 1949 and in the early years it was broadcast from amateur dance events held throughout the country with Syd Perkins and Edna Duffield, two professional dancers, teaching amateur dancers how to dance properly.

In 1953 the competitive element to the show was introduced with regional teams competing for the Come Dancing trophy. The programme officially ended in 1995, by which time it was the longest-running British television show in history, although it has since been overtaken by Panorama. It briefly returned for two specials in 1996, and another two in 1998.

During the 1950s the presenters were McDonald Hobley, Peter Dimmock, Sylvia Peters, Peter West, Brian Johnston and Peter Haigh. Later on such famous names included Jimmy Young, Pete Murray, Terry Wogan, Angela Rippon, Michael Aspel, Judith Chalmers, David Jacobs, Charles Nove and Rosemarie Ford.

The Presenters

Above Angela Rippon in 1978 at an awards ceremony. The most shocking thing about this photo is there are TWO Kermit the Frogs!

Above right Pete Murray at home in 1961, around the time he presented Come Dancing

Right Terry Wogan gets in the mood for his new compere job on Come Dancing in 1972

Above Michael Aspel in 1974

Right Charles Nove, far left, with dancers from Come Dancing in 1985

Opposite David Jacobs at his home in Kensington in December 1969

Pan's People, after some personnel
changes, in April 1975. Pictured are
Cherry Gillespie, Sue Menhenick, Babs
Lord, Ruth Pearson and Dee Dee Wilde

Top Of The Pops

A show like Top Of The Pops could not exist without dancing. Originally broadcast each week starting on January 1, 1964, it was traditionally shown every Thursday evening on BBC1, except for a short period on Fridays in late 1974, before being again moved to Fridays in 1996, and then to Sundays on BBC Two in 2005. It finally ended in July 2006, and despite running for 42 years it still did not outlast Come Dancing for longevity!

Besides the studio audience dancing enthusiastically to whoever was appearing on that week's show, the BBC decided it needed some professionals to dance to a song when an artist could not appear or to accompany other artists. The first professionals were known as the Go-Jos after Jo Cook who put the troupe together.

Initially, Linda Hotchkin and Jane Bartlett were the two other members of the Go-Jos. When Jo Cook decided to

The original Pan's People members arrive at Heathrow in November 1971. Clockwise from top left, Louise Clarke, Flick Colby, Andi Rutherford, Babs Lord, Dee Dee Wilde and Ruth Pearson

concentrate on choreography they expanded to six with the addition of Lesley Larbey, Wendy Hilhouse, Barbara van der Heyde and Thelma Bignell.

The dance group that everyone remembers is, of course, Pan's People who first appeared on TOTP in May 1968. They did not start off with weekly appearances but became an almost-weekly feature of the programme by early 1970. Pan's People were not formed specifically for TOTP and had been a dance group for several years before their first appearance. Two dancers, Dee Dee Wilde and Ruth Pearson, from the troupe were invited to dance on TOTP by choreographer Virginia Mason in 1968 for a routine to Simon Says by the 1910 Fruitgum Company. This was followed by a further routine featuring three members of Pan's People, Dee Dee, Ruth and Flick Colby, dancing to Respect by Aretha Franklin, and subsequently, the entire sextet appeared in a routine set to US Male by Elvis Presley. The other three dancers were Louise Clarke, Babs Lord and Andi Rutherford. Pan's People made their final TOTP appearance in April 1976. There followed a string of dance groups including Ruby Flipper, Legs & Co. and Zoo.

"DESPITE RUNNING FOR 42 YEARS TOP OF THE POPS STILL DID NOT OUTLAST COME DANCING FOR LONGEVITY!"

Dee Dee Wilde, Babs Lord and Louise Clarke in 1969

Ready, Steady, Go!

The television show that was very epitome of the swinging sixties was first broadcast in August 1963 from TV House in London's Kingsway. The show was broadcasting on a Friday evening with the slogan of 'The Weekend Starts Here'. It became synonymous with the era. RSG! was Britain's weekly look at the 'fab, happening scene' in London; it shaped the taste of the nation.

RSG! was hosted by former Cambridge law student Keith Fordyce and the woman who became known as the 'Queen of the Mods', Cathy McGowan. Cathy became an icon of pop culture, telling viewers what was in or out, hot or not. She also gave credence to the concept that anyone could make it, rubbing shoulders with the stars and even becoming their friend. Cathy had worked in the office of the TV company and was later quoted as saying, "I blundered my way through each show."

When it started the show had two resident dancers, Theresa Confrey and Patrick Kerr, who demonstrated the latest dances, alongside the 'hand-picked' studio audience. Scouts from the show went to clubs throughout London, like the Sabre and Crawdaddy, offering the best dancers free tickets to the show.

From April 1965, RSG! was live and broadcast from Wembley rather than Kingsway. The programme ran for 175 episodes until December 1966. The very premise on which the programme was built was being overtaken by a new era of beads, hair and granny glasses. The beat boom and the Mod generation had finally lost ground to the Age of Aquarius.

> "SCOUTS FROM THE SHOW WENT TO CLUBS THROUGHOUT LONDON, LIKE THE SABRE AND CRAWDADDY, OFFERING THE BEST DANCERS FREE TICKETS TO THE SHOW"

Above and Left
Ready, Steady Go! dancers in February 1964. What's interesting is that it was a multi-racial show ahead of its time. It gave over a whole show to visiting Tamla Motown stars that was compered by Dusty Springfield. Seeing those Motown acts do the choreographed routines was a revelation

Above The Beatles on Ready, Steady, Go! in March 1964, naturally with dancers

Right Ringo Starr interviewed by hostess Cathy McGowan on the set of TV show Ready, Steady, Go! in March 1964

Copacabana

B arry Manilow released Copacabana in the immediate aftermath of the disco craze and it harks back to an earlier era of glitz and glamour, of Astaire and Rogers and everything that I love about ballroom and Latin dancing.

The idea for the song was inspired by a conversation between Manilow and Bruce Sussman at the Copacabana Hotel in Rio de Janeiro, the same hotel that featured in the 1933 film Flying Down to Rio. Neither, Manilow or Sussman could remember if there was already a song called 'Copacabana' and so when the singer returned to New York they checked it out, found there wasn't and decided to write one.

Manilow, who had been a regular visitor to the Copacabana nightclub in New York City, wrote the music and Sussman and Jack Feldman wrote the lyrics. It made the US top 10 but surprisingly failed to make the Top 40 in Britain, but became Manilow's first gold single for a song won a Grammy Award for Pop Male Vocalist in February 1979.

In 1985, Manilow expanded the song into a full length, made-for-television musical, adding new songs to the plot suggested by the song. This was then transformed into a full-length, two-act stage musical that ran at the Prince of Wales Theatre on London's West End for two years prior to a lengthy tour of the UK. An American production was later mounted that toured the US for over a year.

Above Barry Manilow performing in Copacabana in 1996

SONGS THAT GOT BRITAIN DANCING

Thriller

Thriller, the song, as featured in the 13-minute mini movie/video is the most influential pop video of all time. It took creativity in video-making to a whole new level, and it is the dancing in particular that makes this such a sensational film. Seeing the choreography and Michael Jackson's brilliant dancing for the first time was one of the most exciting moments in modern dance – it took everything to a whole new level.

Jackson's dancing was influenced by all the greats, including Gene Kelly, Fred Astaire, Bob Fosse, James Brown, and Sammy Davis Jr. as well as The Nicholas Brothers. According to Jackson, "When I saw him move I was mesmerized. I've never seen a performer perform like James Brown and right then and there I knew that that was what I wanted to do for the rest of my life." He also dedicated his autobiography, Moonwalk, to Fred Astaire. After a 1983 TV performance of Billie Jean, Astaire called Jackson and said, "I watched it last night, and I taped it, and I watched it again this morning. You're a helluva mover. You put the audience on their ASS last night!"

There are any number of movies and TV shows where the dancing directly influenced Michael, including Fred Astaire in Top Hat, Swing Time, Band Wagon and Royal Wedding.

There was Bill Bailey from Showtime at the Apollo, James Brown in the TAMI Show from 1965 and John W. Sublett, nicknamed Bubbles from Cabin In The Sky.

The Thriller video was directed by John Landis, who worked on the 1981 movie An American Werewolf In London, and this was certainly where some of the influence came from, but the dancing was revolutionary, it transformed the way we thought about modern dance. The graveyard dance started the trend of group dance scenes in pop videos, forcing other performers who were not nearly as adept as Jackson to somehow incorporate dance into what they do. Now everyone does it.

What you may not know is that Thriller was not written by Michael Jackson but by Rod Temperton, who comes from Cleethorpes in Lincolnshire and was originally in the band Heatwave, who had some disco hits in the 1970s. In 1979, producer Quincy Jones asked Temperton to write songs for what became Michael Jackson's first solo album, Off The Wall.

Michael Jackson is pictured performing on stage at Wembley in July 1988

Sunday Night At The London Palladium

S unday Night At The London Palladium is the epitome of a British television variety show. It ran on ITV from 1955 to 1967, with a brief revival in 1973 and 1974, and in September 2014 it was revived again. You just can't keep a good brand down!

Every artists wanted to appear on the programme and it regularly featured dancers that included the famous high-kicking Tiller Girls. It had a number of presenters over the years including Tommy Trinder (1955–1958), Norman Vaughan (1962–1965, 1974), Jimmy Tarbuck (1965–67) and of course, Bruce Forsyth (1957–1960 and 1961–64).

Above The famous Tiller Girls in May 1960

Right Bruce Forsyth with the cast from Sunday Night At The London Palladium in 1957

Brucie bows out...

I couldn't finish this book without paying tribute to Sir Bruce Forsyth and, through him, all the other old-school variety performers that included song and dance in their act.

Fact is, if you wanted to be an all-round entertainer then you had to be able to dance and, as Bruce proved every week on Strictly, he could certainly do that.

Born in Edmonton, North London in 1928, Bruce is acknowledged as having the longest-running television career of any entertainer.

He's hosted so many TV shows it's impossible to list even a few of them to do him credit but you can always expect Bruce to break into a little dance routine. I remember one Strictly Christmas special where we had some major technical problems a few years ago. Bruce went out and entertained the audience with songs, jokes and dancing. He is a real trooper, and if anyone deserves the title 'Living Legend' it's Brucie!

And may I say Bruce, "keep dancing!"

Left
Bruce Forsyth at
the Royal Albert
Hall in London

Below left
As a young boy
sometime in the
1930s

Right
Bruce, Nyree
Dawn Porter,
and Lionel Blair
rehearsing for a
TV show in July
1969

Below
In 1961 with his
co-star from the
pantomime Turn
Again Whittington

Rehearsing for the Royal Variety Performance in May 1960

Above Two legends. One of the most gifted song and dance men, Sammy Davis Jr, with Bruce in September 1980

Right Bruce with his Bafta fellowship award in 2008

Below With the Aleta Morrison Dancers

Agadoo

Recorded by Black Lace in 1984, Agadoo peaked at No.2 in the charts and became the eighth best-selling single of 1984 in the UK. It's been voted the fourth most annoying song of all time and been described as, "sounding like the school disco you were forced to attend, your middle-aged relatives forming a conga at a wedding party… every party cliché you ever heard".

Oops Upside Your Head

Party record, novelty record or dance record? It's all of these and more. It's one of those records that just seemed to capture the public's imagination when it was released in the summer of 1980. The Gap Band had already released three albums before The Gap Band II, their fourth album from which Oops Upside Your Head was taken.

For some inexplicable reason when it hit the clubs, people started dancing to it. I say dancing but in fact they sat on the floor and did this kind of a dance in rows and that included a rhythmic rowing action. Well, as I've always said, it doesn't matter what gets people dancing, just as long as they do.

It is just another record that spawned a dance craze, one of many. Here's some others that you may remember.

Black Lace celebrating being selected to represent the UK at the Eurovision Song Contest; they came seventh!

The Time Warp

The song featured in the 1973 rock musical The Rocky Horror Show and in the 1975 film adaptation The Rocky Horror Picture Show. It is a parody of the dance song genre in which much of the content of the song is given over to dance step instructions. When the film is screened the audiences are known to get up and dance, The Time Warp, but it has also become one of those wedding disco classics!

Richard O'Brien, who starred in the musical The Rocky Horror Show

The Chicken Dance

Which we know and love as 'The Birdie Song' is an oom-pah song that was composed by accordion player Werner Thomas from Davos, Switzerland, in the 1950s. The name of the original Swiss song was Der Ententanz (The Duck Dance). In 1981 Henry Hadaway produced 'The Birdie Song' by The Tweets and it reached No.2 in the UK singles chart in October 1981. In 2000 it was voted "the most annoying song of all time" in a poll but it didn't stop it being danced at thousands, tens of thousands, maybe more wedding discos.

"SHAPE A BEAK WITH YOUR HANDS... MAKE CHICKEN WINGS WITH YOUR ARMS"

How to do the Chicken Dance:

• At the start of the music, shape a chicken beak with your hands. Open and close them four times, during the first four beats of the music.
• Make chicken wings with your arms. Flap your wings four times, during the next four beats of the music.
• Make a chicken's tail feathers with your arms and hands. Wiggle downwards during the next four beats of the music.
• Clap four times during the next four beats of the music while rising to your feet.
• Repeat this process four times.
• At the bridge, hold your arms straight, in imitation of an aircraft. All dancers spin around the room in "flight" until the bridge ends.

But remember, only in the privacy of your own home…

Rehearsing for the final of series eight of Strictly Come Dancing in December 2010

Strictly speaking, it's been wonderful

How did I end up on the TV talking about "all sausage, no sizzle"? Well it's too long a story for here, but I just wanted to share a little bit of the magic of being on Strictly Come Dancing with you. The first ever Strictly show was in 2004, which means it's been ten years of sitting on the judging panel watching amateurs become almost as good as professionals and professionals teaching people, that never thought they could ever dance, to perform what are, in some cases, minor miracles. It really has been a privilege.

"SINCE THE FIRST SERIES THINGS SEEMED TO HAVE GOT MORE GLITZY AND GLAMOROUS"

Above *Strictly Come Dancing Roadshow at the Scottish Exhibition and Conference Centre in Glasgow in 2008*

Opposite *Sir Bruce Forsyth in September 2012*

Seven!

Strictly Come Dancing has done more to get people in Britain once again doing ballroom and Latin dancing than anything else could ever have done. When I worked on the pilot show and during the early part of the first series what I cared about most was that dancing's image was not tarnished. And what I admire most about the BBC is that they didn't poke it away at 10.35pm on a Tuesday evening they went for it, big time – it had the glitz and the glamour of a full-scale production.

Of course I need not have worried. People have taken it into their hearts and since the first series things seemed to have got more glitzy and glamorous as each series has come along.

In 2008 we did our first Strictly Come Dancing live tour around arenas in Britain and it was a sell out, as every tour has been since. While it is always fun in the studio filming Strictly it is so great to meet people and hear just how supportive of the dancers the audiences are.

➤

Even during the filming of the TV series we did some shows outside of the BBC's Television Centre. In 2004 we went to Blackpool Tower and returned there several times. In 2011 and 2012 we went to Wembley and did the programme live from there. It was a massive logistical undertaking and I take my hat off to the production crew for the brilliant job they do in putting such a seamless show together

After eleven series of the show we've had five women who have won and six men, so I'm wondering will our twelfth series even things up?

What a trooper! Russell Grant about to be shot out of the giant cannon at Wembley in November 2011

Theses gymnasts were part of the Wembley show and, like the professional dancers, they are professional in everything they do. The professionals are the stars of the show

The complexity of the production is mind-blowing. I've only just mastered an iPad!

CAM1 CAM2 CAM3 CAM4
CAM5 CAM6 CAM7 CAM8
CAM10 CAM11

"IT WAS A MASSIVE LOGISTICAL UNDERTAKING AND I TAKE MY HAT OFF TO THE PRODUCTION CREW FOR THE BRILLIANT JOB"

Bruno Tonioli and me behind the scenes at Wembley Arena during rehearsals for the live show in November 2011

Dancing Queen

Benny Andersson, Anni-Frid Lyngstad (Frida), Agnetha Fältskog and Björn Ulvaeus in February 1978

A perfect pop song that somehow unites everyone in a love of music and, of course, in dancing. It's like all the great Motown records, it has an intro that commands your attention from the moment it starts. Released in August 1976, it was recorded a year earlier, and it was one of the most successful singles of the 1970s.

Dancing Queen was written by Benny Andersson, Björn Ulvaeus and Stig Anderson, and features the shared lead vocal of Agnetha Fältskog and Anni-Frid Lyngstad.

It took some of its inspiration from the dance rhythm in George McCrae's Rock Your Baby, and more unusually from the drumming on New Orleans's legend, Dr. John's 1972 album Dr. John's Gumbo.

The group all knew that it was a hit long before it was released, according to Benny "it's one of those songs where you know during the sessions that it's going to be a smash hit". While Agnetha has said, "It's often difficult to know what will be a hit. The exception was Dancing Queen. We all knew it was going to be massive".

They don't come any bigger. It topped the charts in more than a dozen countries including Sweden (where it spent 14 weeks at No.1), Australia, Belgium, Brazil, West Germany, Ireland, Mexico, the Netherlands, New Zealand, Norway, South Africa and Rhodesia and of course the UK. Dancing Queen also topped the charts in the America and became, ABBA's only No.1 on the U.S Hot 100.

> "A PERFECT POP SONG THAT SOMEHOW UNITES EVERYONE IN A LOVE OF MUSIC AND OF COURSE IN DANCING"

Top Abba's members on Brighton beach the day before the Eurovision Song Contest in 1974, which they won performing Waterloo

Above The 1974 Eurovision Song Contest contestants outside the Royal Pavilion in Brighton

Ten!

As I've said I admire the dancers, both amateur and professional, for the commitment they show on Strictly, and none more so than the winners. In the three-month journey from the first week's show to the final the effort that is required to win the series is incredible. Of course, there is a little luck involved sometimes, just like there is a little bad luck for those who don't win the final. But as we all now know, it takes a lotta tens to win Strictly!

Victoria Pendleton and Louis Smith before the start of series ten in September 2012. Louis and his partner Flavia Cacace eventually won the three-way final with Kimberley Walsh and Pasha Kovalev, and Denise van Outen and James Jordan. Remarkably, all three of their dances were awarded 10 by all four judges, except, ironically Louis who got a nine from Craig for his Charleston

"AS WE ALL NOW KNOW, IT TAKES A LOTTA TENS TO WIN STRICTLY!"

Left Darren Gough and Lilia Kopylova. When I looked at the list of celebrities before the start of series three I thought, Darren? He's likely to be a Yorkshire pudding, but he turned into a Yorkshire terrier

Below Jill Halfpenny and Darren Bennett who won series two. They did the most brilliant jive for which they deservedly got four tens

Kara Tointon and Artem Chigvintsev won series eight, despite me only giving them a seven for their American Smooth

Tom Chambers and Camilla Dallerup, the winners of series six in which the final two celebrities were Rachel Stevens and Tom. It was a close call and Rachel was probably the better all rounder, but Tom produced the most fantastic freestyle performance it had everything – good technique and high performance level

Left Chris Hollins and Ola Jordan, the winners of series seven, rehearsing at the Dance Academy, Battersea. It was a close call between Ricky Whittle and Chris as to who would win but four tens on the Charleston nailed it for Chris and Ola

It's not the winning, it's the taking part! You've got to hand it to Robbie Savage, who along with his partner Ola Jordan were knocked out of series nine in week ten. It takes guts to go and dance during half-time at Madejski Stadium at the Reading and Derby County match in October 2011

The last song's just been played
and it's time to go. I hope you
enjoyed that as much as I did.
Stay happy and...

keep dancing!

Len Goodman

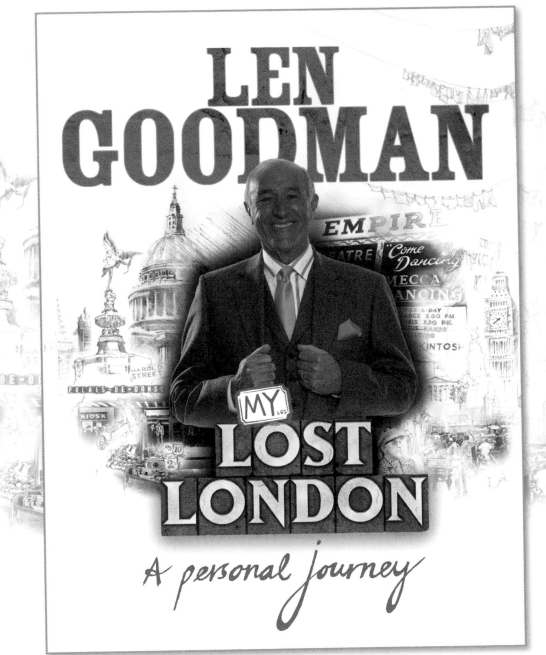